Wild Goose big book *of* liturgies

Volume 2

Wild Goose big book *of* liturgies Volume 2

wild goose
publications
www.ionabooks.com

Published 2018 by
Wild Goose Publications
21 Carlton Court, Glasgow G5 9JP, UK,
the publishing division of the Iona Community.
Scottish Charity No. SC003794. Limited Company Reg. No. SC096243.

ISBN 978-1-84952-616-6

Overseas distribution
Australia: Willow Connection Pty Ltd, Unit 4A, 3–9 Kenneth Road, Manly Vale, NSW 2093
New Zealand: Pleroma, Higginson Street, Otane 4170, Central Hawkes Bay
Canada: Bayard Distribution, 10 Lower Spadina Ave., Suite 400, Toronto, Ontario M5V 2Z

Printed by Bell & Bain, Thornliebank, Glasgow

Contents

The same old way?

A liturgy for a new year

Thom M Shuman

Call to worship:

We wake up in the morning
and see the sunrise:
How majestic is your name in all the earth!

We are warmed by the sun;
the rain cleanses all creation:
How majestic is your name in all the earth!

We watch the moon light up the night;
we fall asleep to the lullabies of the stars:
How majestic is your name in all the earth!

Prayer:

You call us
to be your children;
you gift us
to serve all people;
you send us to proclaim
your good news to all:
glory to you,
Creator of all that is new.

When you are lonely,
we have a chance to visit you;
when you are hungry,
we can share our food with you;
when you are naked,
we can give you
the clothes off our back;
when you are sick,
we can nurse you back to health:
glory to you,
Saviour of the world.

You whisper in our ears,
so we may praise you;

you fill our souls,
so we may serve you;
you lead us into the kingdom,
so we may live with you:
glory to you,
Spirit of gentleness.

Glory to you,
God in Community, Holy and One.
Hear us as we pray as Jesus teaches us …

Lord's Prayer

Call to reconciliation:

Will this year be a time of new life, new ways for us –
or will we continue to live the same old way? …

Let us confess to God our failures, as well as our hopes,
as we begin this new year …

Song

Prayer for forgiveness:

God of every moment,
we admit that we always find the time
to fill our stomachs,
but not our souls.
We spend hours watching television,
but not the wonders of your creation.
We arrange outings with our friends,
yet ignore your invitation to sit and talk.
We make resolutions to change every aspect of our lives,
except for that which pertains to you.
Forgive us, God of glory,

and make us new.
In the moments to come this year,
remind us that if there is indeed 'a time for everything',
then we *do* have those moments to spend in grace,
seeking hope, finding joy,
and for a relationship with our Lord and Saviour,
Jesus Christ.

Silence

Assurance of pardon:

It's over – last year is gone.
Our words, our thoughts, our deeds are in the past.
Today, we begin anew.
Today, and every day, God offers us life and hope.

Here, now, forever – we are forgiven and healed.
Let this year be the year we will live as such people.
Thanks be to God!
Amen

Prayer of dedication:

May we not keep our blessings,
but give them away:
so that others might learn new dance steps,
so children might be fed,
so bridges might be built
and so grace may flow to all in your world.
In Jesus' name, we pray.
Amen

Offering

Suggested Bible readings: Psalm 8, Ecclesiastes 3:1–13, Matthew 25:31–46, Revelation 21:1–6a

Song

Reflection:

When I woke this
morning,
I would have slipped
into that crisp, starched
button-down-collar
dress shirt
I gifted to myself
but
you hand me that robe
you wore when
you fed the 5000
on the hillside;

you slip my feet
into those sandals
worn smooth by
your journeys
up and down
the streets of the
kingdom;

around my waist
you wrap that towel
still showing the heels
of the feet of your
friends
washed in your tears
on that night so long
ago;

looking at me
from head to foot,
you nod,
whispering,

'*Now* you're ready
for the New Year.'

Or:

I've been working on my list of New Year resolutions: walk more; eat more fruit and fibre, less fat; lose that 'spare tyre' around the middle (though now it's more like a complete set!). And you know what I noticed? It's the same list I had in 2016. In fact, it's the same list I had in 2006, 1996, 1986, 1976 …

It's always the same old things I am working at improving. There is no new thing on my list – that activity I have never tried, that event I have never attended, that place I have never visited.

We fall into the trap of thinking God uses the same list year after year, that God will always do things the way they have always been done. Yet, the New Testament reminds us that God is in the business of newness: new heaven, new earth, new Jerusalem, new me, new you.

It shouldn't surprise us though. Scripture makes it clear that God is always willing to risk, to dare, to think and do outside the box – to do something, everything new! And God wants us to be open to that new thing offered to us, to that new person who will enhance our life, to that new challenge which will make us grow, to that new opportunity we will have to serve. So let's tear up all our old, dated lists and be open to that one new thing (probably more, but let's start with one) that God will do for us, to us, through us.

Song

Great prayer of thanksgiving:

May the God of new beginnings be with you.
And also with you.

People of God, lift up your hearts.
We lift them to the one who makes all things,
including us, new.

Children of God, sing praises to the one who gives new life.
We praise the one who continues to surprise us
with hope and grace.

Before there was time,
Hope of Eternity,
you took a moment
to bring creation out of chaos.
You took time to create mountains
and carve deep canyons;
you made the time to fill the oceans
and to give food for all creatures;
you found the time to plough rivers,
to water a garden,
and to shape us in your image.

But we did not have time for you,
preferring to spend our days chasing sin,
and our nights seeking death.
You always made time for us,
speaking of your hopes
through the prophets,
sharing your dreams
through the angels.

Then, one day you decided
to do a new thing:
becoming one of us
as Jesus become human,
to bring hope and grace.

So we join with the saints in heaven,
and our sisters and brothers on earth,
who sing of your glory:

Holy, holy, holy God of every time and space.
All creation sings of your majesty and glory.
Hosanna in the highest!

Blessed is the one who gives us the water of life.
Hosanna in the highest!

Holy are you, Keeper of our days,
and blessed is Jesus Christ,
who is with us in every season of life.
He comes not to judge us,
but to forgive us;
he comes not to cast us out,
but to gather us into
the New Jerusalem;
he comes not to watch us suffer,
but to die on the cross,
that we might live with you.
As we give thanks for his life,
and remember his death and resurrection,
we talk of that mystery which is our faith:

Christ died,
so sin would have no more power over us.

Christ rose,
destroying death's grip on us.

When the new heaven and new earth come
Christ will make all things, including us, new.

In these sacred moments,
send your Spirit
to sanctify the bread and the cup,
and to open the hearts
of those who approach the table.

As the Bread of life touches our lips,
may we be strengthened to serve
those the world has forgotten.

As the Cup of salvation quenches our thirst for you,
may we be enabled to bring relief

to those who wander
the desert wastes of our society.

And when all time ends,
and all people are gathered
around your Table in heaven,
we will rejoice in your presence
and sing your praises forever:
One God,
Father, Son and Holy Spirit,
now and forever. Amen

Sending:

Let us go from this time of silence and song
to be God's voice:
To speak out for the oppressed of our communities and the world.

Let us go from this time of community
to be Jesus' faithful:
To feed the hungry,
to visit the sick,
to be a friend to prisoners.

Let us go from this sacred space
to share the peace of the Spirit:
To work for reconciliation in our neighbourhoods,
to put an end to violence and death.

Blessing

The best gift ever

An all-age service for worshipping with the Magi

Nancy Cocks

For this service, everyone needs a paper heart big enough to write a few words on or draw a little picture. Have pencils or markers nearby.

Opening responses:

With each new day
There is a new beginning.

With each new year
We can make a fresh start.

With a fresh start and a new beginning
There is fresh hope.

With fresh hope in our hearts
We come to worship God.

Hymn: 'Shine, Jesus, shine' (various songbooks)

Our prayer to greet God:

God of light and love, we gather in wonder to praise you for the bright sun that makes the snow sparkle and for the twinkling stars which light up the night sky. We praise you for the love we share in smiles that sparkle and eyes that twinkle. Most of all we praise you for Jesus, the Light of the world. His love shines into our lives to warm our hearts and guide our footsteps. Shine on us today, O God, so we remember to follow Jesus every day of this new year.

We say sorry to God (said all together):

God of angels and the wise Magi,
you know we don't always act like angels.
We say the wrong thing and someone gets hurt.
We're not always wise either.
We do something foolish

and we don't know how to set things right.
Jesus, we're sorry.
Help us make a fresh start in this new year.
Guide us by the love that shines from your life.

We hear a kind word from Jesus:

Remember Jesus said, *'I am the Light of the world. Whoever follows me will never walk in darkness but will have the light of life.'* When we say sorry to God from the bottom of our hearts, Jesus will light up our lives with his love. This is very good news!

Sung response: sing through the chorus of 'Shine, Jesus, shine' again

The best gift ever:

Worship leader in conversational style:

Tell me about your favourite Christmas present this year ...

When you think about all the presents you really like, is there one you might call your best gift ever? ...

The worship leader might give an example from childhood of a wonderful gift.

This Sunday's Bible story tells us about the presents Jesus received when he was born.

Bible reading: Matthew 2:1–12

Or choose a retelling of the story of the Magi's visit to Jesus, appropriate for the ages of the children gathered. Emphasise the amazing gifts – not so much about Herod's worry!

Worship leader:

Gold and frankincense and myrrh – these are very unusual gifts for a baby. Not like toys to cuddle or new clothes for a baby to wear.

We know gold is very precious and very expensive;
it's very heavy and very important.
Even today a gift of gold is still a real treasure.
So gold was a great gift to give a new king.
Frankincense and myrrh are oils that are very rare
and make the air smell beautiful when you breathe in.
It's like giving a gift of very special perfume –
even today a tiny bottle of perfume can cost hundreds of dollars –
so perfume can be a real treasure, too.
The gifts from the Magi were pretty lovely gifts for a new king, too.
Gold, frankincense and myrrh.
These were gifts fit for a king,
treasures to honour Jesus, who is our king, too.

So now let's sing the story of the star and the three magi who were called kings themselves, and those wonderful gifts they brought for Jesus, our king.

Song: 'We three kings' (various songbooks)

Worship leader in conversational style:

How do you choose a gift for someone? …

What do you think about when you're picking a gift for your mum or dad? A friend? …

Story: Just what I wanted (Sherman the dog gets the perfect gift)

The story can be read by one reader, or with parts shared around.

'I love Christmas,' Sherman said as he sniffed around the Christmas tree on Christmas Eve. There were lots of presents, wrapped and waiting for Christmas morning. 'Lots of cookies to eat and fancy paper to chew. Is there something for me?' He sniffed some more.

'Sherman, get away from the tree,' said Lucy when she walked into the room. 'No peeking before Christmas morning.'

'Did you get me something?' he asked.

'Of course I got you a present,' said Lucy. 'I got something for everybody.'

'I hope you didn't get me a leash,' Sherman frowned. 'For me getting a leash is like you getting socks for Christmas. No fun at all.'

Lucy smiled. 'I thought about getting you a kitten to chase.'

'A cat! Not a cat! That would be like you getting an extra big brother for Christmas,' Sherman moaned.

Lucy made a face. 'One brother is more than enough – any day of the year. I got you the perfect gift. You'll just have to wait and see.'

On Christmas morning, everybody gathered around the tree. Mark started to hand out presents, one at a time, so everybody could watch while someone opened their gift.

'Hurry up,' Sherman whined. 'I want to see my perfect gift.'

Mark sorted through a few gifts. 'OK, OK,' he said. 'Here it is.' Sherman's present was long and thin, and lumpy.

'It's not the right shape to be a TV for the doghouse. You know, I could be a real watchdog with my own TV.' Sherman grabbed the present and shook it hard. The ribbon flew off and the paper ripped.

And there it was. A brand-new leather slipper.

'So you don't have to eat Mark's old slippers any more,' Lucy announced.

'Gee, thanks, Lucy. It's just what I wanted. I've never had my own slipper before. But how come there's only one slipper?'

'My friend Marsha took the other slipper home for her dog Princess. One week we each spent half our allowance on that pair of slippers. So you and Princess each get half a pair this Christmas.'

Sherman gave the slipper a good, hard shake. 'Better snap than Mark's old slipper.' He shook his head once more and let the slipper sail across the living room. 'Flies better, too!'

Then Sherman sniffed the new slipper. 'But it doesn't smell like that old slipper.'

'Of course not,' said Lucy. 'It's brand new. Mark hasn't put his stinky old feet in it.'

'Too bad,' Sherman said. 'Dogs love stinky old feet!'

Later that morning, once all the presents were opened, while Mark and Lucy were busy with their presents, Sherman decided to bury his new slipper in the garden.

'After a few days in the dirt, it will smell like a real slipper.'

So he went outside and dug a hole beside a rosebush in the backyard, next to where he'd buried his favourite bone the week before. 'By next week this slipper will taste like my bone. Yum!'

Then Sherman went to find Mark's old slipper, the one he'd been chewing on before Christmas. He looked in his doghouse. No slipper. He looked under the couch. No slipper. 'Maybe Mark is wearing it again.' So Sherman went to check Mark's bedroom.

As Sherman pawed through the shoes in the closet, he felt a hand on his collar. 'What are you after? You've got your own slipper now. Leave mine alone,' Mark said, frowning.

'But I'm looking for your old slipper. You know, the one I was chewing last week. You remember. I made a hole in the toe so you could get a new pair.'

'Sure, I remember. I think Mum threw that slipper out. She knew you were getting a new one. She figured the old one was no good any more.'

'No good any more! How could she throw out my old slipper? It tasted so good. It smelled so good. I loved that old slipper.'

'So did I – before you ate it. You'll just have to play with your new one. Where did you hide it?'

Sherman hung his head. 'I buried it.'

'A brand-new slipper? Why did you bury your new slipper?'

'So it would taste as good as the old one. New slippers need a bit of dirt. For flavour.' Sherman sniffed fondly at the shoes in Mark's closet. 'Could I borrow one of your sneakers until my new slipper is ready? There's plenty of dirt on your sneakers already.'

Mark shrugged. 'But then what will I wear?'

While Mark was thinking about his shoes, Sherman grabbed a sneaker and dashed out the bedroom door.

'Come back here, you sneaky old dog!' Mark called.

'Why do you think they call them sneakers?' Sherman asked. By then, he was already under Lucy's bed, hard at work on another toe!

Worship leader in conversational style:

Sherman's story helps us think about how to give someone just what they hoped for, something that might turn out to be the best gift ever.

At the beginning of a new year, it's a good time to think about how to choose a gift we can give to God this year.

What kind of gift tells God that God is important to us? …

What kind of gift shows God our love? …

Gifts from the heart:

Ask everyone to take a paper heart. Talk about a gift from the heart. Something given with us in mind. Something given with love. Something just right …

Leader: On your heart write or draw something you can give God this year. Something given with love, with God in mind, just right. A kind of New Year's resolution from the heart.

Give people a few minutes to write or draw on their hearts. The hearts will be collected with the offering, in the same offering plates or in a second set of plates.

The Offering:

Leader: Now we give our gifts to God …

The offering is received.

We sing our thank you to God:

What can I give Him, poor as I am?
If I were a shepherd, I would bring a lamb;
If I were a Wise Man, I would do my part;
Yet what I can I give Him: give my heart.

From 'In the Bleak Midwinter' (various songbooks)

Prayers from our hearts:

Voice one: God of all time and space, God of the stars and the moon …

Voice two: God of miracle and manger, God of wise men and good friends …

Voice one: We pray that the worship we share in Jesus' name may lead us to act for goodness in the lives and places we touch. May the songs we sing help others to sing, even if they are sad.

Leader: God, you gave us the best gift ever in Jesus.

All: Help us give you a gift from the heart this year.

Voice two: May the gifts we have given and received this Christmas teach us to be generous throughout the coming year. May the stars we hung on our Christmas trees and the stars that hang in the sky remind us that you don't want anyone, no one, to live in darkness in the year ahead.

Leader: God, you gave us the best gift ever in Jesus.

All: Help us give you a gift from the heart this year.

Voice one: In a few moments of silence we offer you the prayers of our hearts, the gifts we want to give you this year …

Silence (about 10 seconds)

Leader: God, you gave us the best gift ever in Jesus.

All: Help us give you a gift from the heart this year.

Voice two: We remember before you with love and concern all the people and places, all the creatures and features of this world that face struggle or fear, sorrow or danger this day. Hold them in your love as we think of their names in silence …

Silence

Leader: God, you gave us the best gift ever in Jesus.

All: Help us give you a gift from the heart this year.

Voice one: Hear these prayers and all the silent prayers of our hearts, O God.

Voice two: And cradle them and us in your holy wisdom for Christ's sake. Amen

Song: 'Reamo Leboga' ('To God our thanks we give') (various songbooks), or another song of thanksgiving

Blessing

One for the baptiser

All-age resources for baptisms and Baptismas (the Feast of the Baptism of Jesus)

Janet Lees

A Baptismas play

I like the word Baptismas – it's both unexpected ('We've never heard of it!') and expected ('Like Christmas: only for Baptism'). I think church is generally far too predictable.

At school we did a bit of creative conversation on Baptismas. What could we have? – Baptismas parties, plays (hence the play here), games, clothes (like camel-hair coats, though not many of them!), food – that was interesting – and included Baptismas cakes; and when one boy got baptised he had one which was blue. We don't celebrate Baptismas and baptisms enough – so go for it.

The Feast of the Baptism of Jesus (Baptismas) usually falls near the beginning of Epiphany, in early January. This can be a good time to renew our baptismal promises together: the promises all Christians make to follow Jesus.

Characters for a Baptismas play could include:

- Narrator
- John the Baptist
- Jesus
- Family/friends of Jesus
- Others: soldiers, people of different ages and backgrounds
- A river: a blue sheet held across the acting area. The cloth can be moved to look like a river and to 'submerge' those being baptised.

There are different ways of approaching a play. Traditional churches do weeks of rehearsals and everyone gets bored; the surprise element is lost and so is the motivation. Alternatively you could base your Baptismas play on a reading from the written Bible, say, Mark 1 (provided here). A narrator could read it out and the parts could be mimed. Or you could 'just go for it'. Invite would-be participants to discuss the action and improvise as you all join in together. It's fine to have additional comments from the larger group of observers if the actors get stuck for what to do or say next. After all, the question 'What was everyone else doing whilst this was going on?' is a good one. Equally, moments of silent reflection while folk all think about what is being presented are also good.

Another idea for an improvised version is to provide some photos of the River Jordan and some paintings depicting Jesus's baptism for the participants to discuss before embarking on the Baptismas play. When we did this we found that there were various things people commented on. Lots of the paintings had a group of people in the background. This gave rise to conversations about the onlookers: who they were, what they might have thought ... Others wondered about what John and Jesus had talked about: previous meetings, a shared childhood, a similar vision for God's work, the experience of being called? ... Some wondered about what it felt like to be baptised (some had been baptised as infants but few had been present at an adult baptism), how cold the water was and so on. All of these points helped the actors to portray the Baptismas story in a unique performance.

Narrator:

This is the Good News about Jesus Christ, the Son of God. It all began as the prophet Isaiah had written:

God said, 'I will send my messenger ahead of you. Someone is shouting in the desert, "Get the road ready for the Lord; make a straight path for him to travel!"'.

John appeared in the desert, baptising people and preaching, 'Turn away from your sins and be baptised and God will forgive you.'

Many people from Judea and the city of Jerusalem went out to hear John. They confessed their sins, and he baptised them in the Jordan River. John wore clothes made of camel's hair, with a leather belt around his waist, and his food was locusts and wild honey.

He said: 'The one who will come after me is much greater than I am. I am not good enough even to bend down and untie his sandals. I baptise you with water, but he will baptise you with the Holy Spirit.'

Soon after that Jesus came from Nazareth in Galilee, and was baptised by John in the Jordan.

When Jesus came up out of the water, he saw heaven opening and the Holy Spirit coming down like a dove. A voice came from heaven,'You are my own dear Son. I am pleased with you.'

Mark 1 (Good News Bible)

Words for Baptismas or baptismal blessings

Come and celebrate! (an invitation)

Come and celebrate with us!
Today we are delighted to be God's people.
Today we are overflowing with what it means
to be called God's children.
Today we are ready to renew our promises
to be part of God's family business.
Today we say 'Yes' to
justice and peace,
love and forgiveness
and the new life of those called
God's own ones.

Making waves (a blessing for the waters of baptism)

We look to you, Wave-maker,
as we admire all the wonders of the universe:
where water, air, earth and fire all make waves
as they reflect your glory.

We look to you, Wave-rider,
as we remember the rocky road,
the ups and downs of the route
you took to Jerusalem.

We look to you, Wave-enhancer,
as we join the cosmic dance,
whirl and pirouette, waltz, tango and jive
with your Spirit in us.

We look to you, the Holy Three in One,
as we take this water,
knowing that you flow through it
as you flow in us.

May it be for *(name)* ever the Life-giver:
refreshing, cleansing and renewing *her/him*,
so that bathed in this water today,
s/he may always be bathed in the waves of your love.

Bless us in water (a blessing for the one/s being baptised)

May we, like Jesus,
live wet:
wet from the waters of chaos
breaking over the earth;
wet from the waters of baptism
breaking over our bodies;
wet from the living water
breaking over our lives.

Bless us in earth, air and fire,
but most of all
bless us in water,
that anointed by the Life-giver
we may follow the way.

Like a penguin (a prayer inviting the presence of the Holy Spirit)

As we admire the dedication of a penguin
struggling to keep a chick warm
and play a part in the whole colony
through the Antarctic winter,
so we welcome the Holy Spirit
who warms us,
enabling us to play our part in this community.

A blessing

Begin by putting a small amount of water in some bowls that can be passed around the group.

Bless the water with prayer and pass it around.

Each person may dip a finger in the water and make the sign of the cross on the back of their hand or on their forehead and receive God's blessing, saying: 'In the name of Jesus. Amen.'

Offer group members the option to pass the bowl on to the next person if they do not wish to participate in the blessing.

Living wet: a song about Jesus's baptism

Tune: 'Meet the Flintstones'

John was just a prophet
who was living in the wilderness.
Wild as a child
he was learning how to eat and dress.
People came to John to be baptised –
a voice in the wilderness he cried:
'Change your ways, repent and
have a wet-wet, wet-wet, wet time;
we'll have a wet time,
we'll have a wet wet time!'

Jesus was John's cousin
and about to start his ministry,
at the River Jordan
who there John was most surprised to see:
'I am just not worthy to untie
your shoes – and look into the sky.'
Down came Holy Spirit –
have a wet-wet, wet-wet, wet time;
we'll have a wet time,
we'll have a wet wet time!

God said: 'This man Jesus,
well he is my most beloved Son.
I am most delighted:
He's the special and the chosen one.'
Come then all you people be baptised.
Jesus is our friend, he is our guide.
When you follow Jesus –
have a wet-wet, wet-wet, wet time;
we'll have a wet time,
we'll have a wet wet time!

Stories and reflections on baptisms

Of course, after all this, it is more than possible that someone will ask to be baptised. Once, a child being adopted into his new family asked if he could be baptised. He was six years old and to him this signalled a new start in his life. He got a new name and a new family to relate to and grow up with. He liked our baptismal song and wanted to have a 'wet wet time' himself. However, he did not choose total immersion baptism (as it's sometimes called). A small amount of water was enough, and less scary, which was fine.

When we did have our first baptism in the swimming pool it was quite an occasion. The water was probably a lot warmer and cleaner than the River Jordan but, like then, the onlookers certainly had plenty to talk about. We began by remembering the story of Jesus's baptism together. Then we heard from Jo, the young person who was being baptised, about her longing to thank God for all the blessings she had received in her life and her desire to follow Jesus. We all knelt by the edge of the pool to bless the water together. As this swimming pool is used every day this gave rise to a number of questions about 'How long would the blessing last?'.

A second part of the service took place in the chapel, where we heard from family and friends encouraging Jo in her discipleship. It was a very moving experience – one still talked about – giving rise to conversations with other young people about their own discipleship. Remember to respond to each young person with careful listening. Children and young people may have heaps of ideas for how they want to celebrate this important step in their faith journey – the time, place, supporters, onlookers or godparents, words, songs, food and more!

One for the baptiser

I can vouch for the fact that the experience of baptising a young person is very moving, and each baptism an important step in the journey of faith for all those involved.

It was awesome.
I held you under the water.
I saw your face disappear
and bubbles rise around you.
I said:
'Jo, I baptise you,
in the name of the Father, the Son and the Holy Spirit.'
It all seemed to happen in slow motion.
Then you bobbed up,
wiping water from your eyes;
we embraced.
I signed you the cross.
I may not wear camel hair
or eat locusts and wild honey
but my whole body was saying
that was also one for the baptiser.

God of desert places

An Ash Wednesday service of taking on and letting go

Rebeka Maples

Introduction:

The season of Lent is a time of preparation. We cannot experience the joy of Easter without first preparing and embarking on the journey that carries us through Lent. Preparation for some begins before Ash Wednesday. Some of the ancient Carnival celebrations went from Christmas until Ash Wednesday. The Mardi Gras in New Orleans harks back to the revelry before the Lenten fast. Some Shrove Tuesday celebrations are still found in Churches on 'Fat' or Pancake Tuesday, remembering times when Christians would 'fatten up' before 40 days of fasting (from Ash Wednesday until Good Friday), not counting Sundays, which some still refer to as 'little Easters'. Today, though, not many Christians consciously prepare for Lent, and fewer attend Ash Wednesday services. It's a shame, because Lent is a reflective and renewing time that touches many different emotions, especially come Holy Week. But we are not there yet. We have a long journey ahead of us, as we walk now with Jesus through our own desert places.

In this service, you are invited to prepare for Lent and make a way for holiness to be a part of your journey through Lent and beyond. Many of us have been here before, at the edge of this wilderness, and for some, this may be our first Lenten journey. But for all of us, we are not the same as we were last year at this time. Life changes and so do we. That is why it is good for us to go on the Lenten journey again, and prepare to sing 'Alleluia' again on Easter morning. But now we must bury our 'Alleluias', as the early Christians did, and prepare for another journey, because we are not there yet.

As we begin our service, the Carnival masks we hide behind must fall. As we come before the One who knows us as we are, we are invited to think about how we will prepare for our 40-day journey.

Worship preparation:

The altar may remain empty, or be set with wilderness items: rocks, sand, bare branches. Keep the atmosphere stark with no flowers or bright colours. The baptismal font or bowl is filled with sand for people to touch to remember the dry places in their lives that they want Jesus to touch. The sand could remain in the font/bowl throughout Lent.

Before the service people receive a notecard, and during the service are invited to write something on the card for which they seek forgiveness, and then to think of a discipline that they will keep during Lent. This may be something to 'take on' (prayer or a mission project) or something to 'give up' (a food item or habit). We use our fast to remind us to turn to God and give thanks, knowing that God forgives us, even us. Thus, by knowing we are forgiven, Lent becomes a joyful season, not one of drudgery and sacrifice. Jesus already made the ultimate sacrifice.

God of desert places

As people enter the church everyone receives a notecard, pen and service sheet. Folk are invited to touch the sand in the baptismal font or bowl: to remember the dry places in their lives that they want Jesus to touch. Quiet music might be played during this.

Welcome:

Introductory words about Lent and the service, with logistics about ashes, and something about writing on the notecard later.

Suggested song: 'This is a day of new beginnings', by Brian Wren, Hope Publishing, or in *The United Methodist Hymnal*, the United Methodist Publishing House, 1989

Opening responses:

Let us prepare now to enter the desert.
We will walk the road that Jesus walked.

Let us celebrate these forty days with songs of praise.
We will fast and pray with Jesus on the way.

Let us remember the times we turned away.
We will confess our sin and turn back to him.

Let us face those desert places in our lives.
We will not go there alone: Jesus has gone there before us.

Face the desert we must, if we are to reach the cross of Easter.
Face the desert we must, but Jesus has gone there before us.

Unison prayer of preparation:

O Lord, throughout these forty days you prayed and kept a fast.
May we do the same, repent and turn to you.
Be with us through all we face and free us from our past;
give us strength that in joy we may follow you,
and see the mystery of your grace shining through at last.
All glory be to you, Christ our King.
Amen

Bible reading: Matthew 4:1–11

Lord, have mercy.
Christ, have mercy.

Reflection:

These or other brief words of reflection may be given:

Now our journey begins: 40 days in the wilderness just like last year, but it is not last year. We are not where we were or who we were last year. Things have happened in our lives and in our world, for better and for worse. Some of us still have the same old habits we had last year, and some of us have experienced new and unexpected changes – babies have been born and loved ones have died. Whatever has happened we are being led by the Spirit into Lent, with all our joys and sorrows, just as Jesus was led into the desert to be tempted by the devil. If we are giving up something for Lent, we are told not to boast about it, and if we are taking on something, Jesus says don't expect praise and admiration. During Lent, we are invited to experience the wilderness alone and spend time praying, but we are not alone. We are never alone: even in our darkest hour, angels come and minister to us, just as they did to Jesus. So the invitation in Lent is to let God touch the things in our lives that are in need of healing. And while we do this, we remember that underneath the dryness of the desert there is water waiting to rise to the surface. It is living water that will refresh us and wash away our sin and sorrow, and give us new life. It is the reward that God promises to give us. It is what makes us fall down on Ash Wednesday, and rise up with joy on Easter morning, because in death and in life, in loneliness and in community, we are always in need of God and each other.

'Ashes, ashes, we all fall down' is a song for giggling children. 'Remember you are dust, and to dust you shall return' is a statement on Ash Wednesday not to remember you will die but that you will live. And the funeral statement 'earth to earth, ashes to ashes, dust to dust' is our assurance in the hope of resurrection.

Ask yourself: what burdens do I carry that I cannot forgive? Sit quietly and allow God to speak to you. Let God carry the burden with you, as you begin the journey from the desert to the cross.

Later in the service you will be invited to write something on your notecard for which you seek forgiveness, and to think of a discipline which will serve as a reminder of God's grace during Lent. There are many spiritual disciplines that will aid in drawing you closer to God. I invite you to choose a practice of doing, or not doing, something that will remind you to turn to God. Choose something that is on your heart – prayer, giving your time or money, reading and meditating on God's Word. Whatever you choose, may it be a time of renewal that carries you through Lent to relive the joy and gift of God's saving grace when you break your fast on Easter morning.

Our ashes, then, are a sign of love and hope, of God's grace etched upon our hearts. 'Return to me,' says the Lord, 'and I will return to you' (Zechariah 1:3). Our Lenten fast is a reminder that God forgives and God's love never leaves us.

Invitation to the Lenten journey: Joel 2:12–15

Lord, have mercy.
Christ, have mercy.

Thanksgiving over the ashes:

Brothers and sisters in Christ, I invite you to observe a holy Lent.
Let us bow in silence before our Creator and Redeemer.

(Brief silence)

The Lord be with you.
And also with you.

Let us pray:

God of desert places,
pray for us now and throughout these forty days.
Grant that these ashes may be a sign
of your presence with us in each season of our lives,
that when the final Easter dawns,
we may join with you in everlasting joy,
and sing praises to your Son,
Jesus Christ our Lord.
Amen

Imposition of ashes:

A hymn or psalm may be sung during this, or ashes may be received in silence. These (or other) words of imposition may be used as each person is marked with a cross of ashes on their forehead, or on the back of their hand:

Come when you are ready and mark the beginning of your Lenten journey …

Remember you are dust, and to dust you shall return.

Repent, and believe the gospel.

Turn to God, and remember that God loves you.

Suggested song: 'Lord, who throughout these forty days', Claudia F. Hernaman, from *The United Methodist Hymnal*, The United Methodist Publishing House, 1989

Psalm of confession:

Psalm 51:1–4,10–12

Lord, have mercy.
Christ, have mercy.

Act of reconciliation:

People are invited to write something on their notecard for which they seek forgiveness, and to think of a discipline which will serve as a reminder of God's grace during Lent …

Our God is merciful and the Source of our salvation,
who desires not that we live in sin or guilt
but rather that we turn from evil,
confess our wrongdoing
and accept forgiveness.
Therefore, may the One who came to restore life
bless you and restore you by the Holy Spirit,
for the living of new life in Christ.
In the name of Jesus Christ, know that you are forgiven.
In the name of Jesus Christ, we know that we are forgiven.

Reception of forgiveness:

As music plays all are invited to bring their card forward and to place it on the altar. The cards are burned outside after the service. Or people keep their card and bring it to the Easter sunrise service to be burned in the 'first fire' of Easter morning.

Reflection:

As we reflect on what we have written on our cards, let us also pray that we may be open to ways that God may speak to us during Lent, through scripture and the actions or words of other people. There are as many ways to pray as there are to live. Sometimes we look for a quiet place, as Jesus did in the garden, and sometimes we want to be with a friend or in a crowd, as Jesus did with his disciples. Sometimes we may read a book or listen to music. Sometimes we may use words and sometimes silence. Whenever and however we pray, we are turning our lives into a prayer and opening ourselves to following God, even to places we would rather not go.

Prayer:

Let us pray together:

God of all love and grace,
we stand at the edge of these forty days,
praying for our sins and accepting your forgiveness,
knowing the commands of Christ and going your way.
And so we pray that Lent will be a time of turning to you,
that your ways will become our ways:

Let us feed the hungry; let us give the thirsty drink;
let us clothe the naked and welcome the stranger;
let us visit those in prison and the sick;
let us tear down walls and build bridges.
Let this be our prayer and our way of life,
so that when all is said and all is done,
we may inherit a place at the table you have prepared for us.
This we pray in the name of the One
who taught us to say when we pray ...

Lord's Prayer

Suggested song: 'The Spirit sends us forth to serve', by Delores Dufner, OCP Publications

Sending forth with blessing:

Love what love can do.
Be all that you can be.
God is calling you.

This is not the past.
Do not live there.
Let the voices go.
Do not cling to what is gone.

This is not the future.
You are not there yet.
Let the worries be.
Do not live where you are not.

This is here and now.
This is all you have.
Do not miss where you are.
For it will not stay for past or future to replay.

Live the life that you are in.
You cannot live where you have been.
You cannot be where you are not.

Be in the time you are in.
Love what you can do.
Be all that you can be.
No one can live for you.
Or be what you can be.

Live and love what love can do.
The time is now.
The place is here.
Love and live what you can do.
God is calling you.

(Pause)

Go now into the desert places where God calls you to go,
and be what God calls you to be.
And may the blessing of Almighty God,
Creator, Son and Holy Spirit,
come upon us and remain with us forever.
Amen

Quiet music or silence

With intuition, imagination and love

A Maundy Thursday service of anointing

Sarah Agnew & Jan Sutch Pickard

Setting: a table in the centre of the worship space with bread, wine, cheese, nuts, dried fruit and lit candles. Before worship you might like to share a group meal.

Ambient music playing.

A leader sounds a singing bowl to begin the service.

Welcome/introduction:

Welcome to Maundy Thursday, to the climax of the story of this Jesus whom we follow. The words of the poems that frame our gathering this evening are on the service sheet, but please feel free simply to listen now and to take the words home for reflection and remembering later; you will hear each poem twice tonight.

There will be a time of silence and reflection after the first reading of each poem. During the second reading of the poems, folk will be invited to anoint one another with water and oil. If you would prefer not to take part in this, that is totally fine.

The closing of our gathering will be somewhat open-ended, leading us into the space of Good Friday. Stay as long as you need or want to once the liturgy is completed. If you would like to linger over coffee or tea and conversation, there will be a space for that in (*the room next door, etc*). Please be mindful of each other as you leave worship, some may want silence …

Gathering words:

We come from different places.
We have different languages for speaking about God:
Sacred, Divine, Holy One ...
We all have a story to tell.
And we all encounter God in the Story in unique ways.

Around this table we commit to listen,
and to respect and affirm each other
and our stories.

Around this table we gather for prayer,
for food,
for friendship –
and we hope to meet God here.

Leader: John 12:1–3 (NRSV)

Six days before the Passover Jesus came to Bethany, the home of Lazarus, whom he had raised from the dead. There they gave a dinner for him. Martha served, and Lazarus was one of those at the table with him. Mary took a pound of costly perfume made of pure nard, anointed Jesus' feet, and wiped them with her hair. The house was filled with the fragrance of the perfume.

Someone brings a bottle of oil to the table.

'Woman with ointment', by Jan Sutch Pickard

To be read by six female voices. Readers are seated in a circle in reading order. Readers speak from a kneeling position.

Female voice 1:

On my knees –
not, for once, scrubbing tiles
or coaxing wax from the chancel carpet;
not arranging flowers
but anointing feet.
By what authority?
Intuition, imagination and love.

Female voice 2:

On my knees –
time and time again:
tying shoelaces,
taking out splinters, counting toes:
is there space in the structures of the Church
for motherly care
and family jokes –
for intuition, imagination, love?

Female voice 3:

On my knees –
getting personal:
coming close, touching, taking risks
of being misunderstood;
filling the air with fragrance, spilling it,
massaging calloused skin,
stiff joints, weary flesh –
how dare I?
Through intuition, imagination, love.

Female voice 4:

On my knees –
where the poor and unnoticed always are:
shining shoes, searching in the gutter,
picking up crumbs.
Right there, on the bottom line,
you will find me, having spent all I had
on this one thing, now pouring it out
extravagantly –
out of intuition, imagination, love.

Female voice 5:

On my knees –
doing something at once symbolic and down-to-earth,
about responsibility, respect
and remembering;
about life and death, ends and beginnings.
A representative person
who is also a human being
in a particular time and place:
frail, fallible, gifted
with intuition, imagination, love.

Female voice 6:

On my knees –
when I'm down here
actions speak louder than words.
But so low (grassroots, shop floor, street level)
you cannot hear my voice;
and when you put me on a pedestal
you cannot see my face.
If we meet somewhere in the middle,
on common ground,
we can serve each other
and rise together –
sharing intuition, imagination, love.

Time of silence and reflection (few minutes)

Leader sounds the singing bowl to close the silence.

Leader: John 13:1,3–5 (NRSV)

Now before the festival of the Passover, Jesus knew that his hour had come to depart from this world and go to the Father. Having loved his own who were in the world, he loved them to the end … Jesus, knowing that the Father had given all things into his hands, and that he had come from God and was going to God, got up from the table, took off his outer robe, and tied a towel around himself. Then he poured water into a basin and began to wash the disciples' feet and to wipe them with the towel that was tied around him.

Someone brings a bowl of water and a towel to the table.

'Jesus anointed, anointing', by Sarah Agnew with the Esther Project Community[1]

To be read by five male voices. Readers are seated in the circle, in between the female readers, in reading order. Readers speak from a kneeling position.

Male voice 1:

On your knees,
where you should not be,
your hair down,
decorum forgotten.
You look up, a brief moment,
your eyes flash
with intuition, imagination, love.

Male voice 2:

On your knees,
while your sister cries in despair
and begs you to stop;

your brother stunned, silent,
you fill the house
with extravagant, fragrant
intuition, imagination and love.

Male voice 3:

On her knees!
He cries for the poor,
though I know more
than I care to see
of this man's hypocrisy –
Judas, my friend, where is
your intuition, imagination, love?

Male voice 4:

On my knees,
anointing their feet,
praying they will
understand
why they are twelve,
their call to serve,
with intuition, imagination, love.

Male voice 5:

On my knees,
in this garden of peace,
I sigh, I groan,
deserted and alone.
I sweat, I ache, I know
these final steps will take my all,
will take much more …

Dear God, Source of my life,
I do this for you, with you
and your intuition, imagination, love.

Time of silence and reflection (few minutes)

Leader sounds the singing bowl to close the silence.

The ritual of anointing:

Leader (pouring oil into the bowl of water while speaking these words):

A bowl of water and fragrant oil. The perfume of Mary's oil filled the whole house with fragrance … and it flowed into the water that Jesus used to wash the disciples' feet. We invite you to offer anointing to one another from the perfume and the water of these acts of love and service.

We will hear the poems together, one stanza at a time, and between each reader the anointing bowl will be passed around. You are invited to kneel, or to remain standing if kneeling is difficult, and to anoint the person on your left *(depending on which way the bowl is passed)*. If you prefer not to take part in the anointing, that is totally fine; please just cross your arms on your chest to indicate that you pass, and remain with us in prayer.

A cantor or small group might lead the singing of a simple chant between readers, or you might choose to leave silence, or a mixture of singing and silence.

Female voice 1:

On my knees –
not, for once, scrubbing tiles
or coaxing wax from the chancel carpet;
not arranging flowers
but anointing feet.
By what authority?
Intuition, imagination and love.

Singing/silence

Male voice 1:

On your knees,
where you should not be,

your hair down,
decorum forgotten.
You look up, a brief moment,
your eyes flash
with intuition, imagination, love.

Singing/silence

Female voice 2:

On my knees –
time and time again:
tying shoelaces,
taking out splinters, counting toes:
is there space in the structures of the Church
for motherly care
and family jokes –
for intuition, imagination, love?

Singing/silence

Male voice 2:

On your knees,
while your sister cries in despair
and begs you to stop;
your brother stunned, silent,
you fill the house
with extravagant, fragrant
intuition, imagination and love.

Singing/silence

Female voice 3:

On my knees –
getting personal:
coming close, touching, taking risks
of being misunderstood;

filling the air with fragrance, spilling it,
massaging calloused skin,
stiff joints, weary flesh –
how dare I?
Through intuition, imagination, love.

Singing/silence

Male voice 3:

On her knees!
He cries for the poor,
though I know more
than I care to see
of this man's hypocrisy –
Judas, my friend, where is
your intuition, imagination, love?

Singing/silence

Female voice 4:

On my knees –
where the poor and unnoticed always are:
shining shoes, searching in the gutter,
picking up crumbs.
Right there, on the bottom line,
you will find me, having spent all I had
on this one thing, now pouring it out
extravagantly –
out of intuition, imagination, love.

Singing/silence

Male voice 4:

On my knees,
anointing their feet,
praying they will

understand
why they are twelve,
their call to serve,
with intuition, imagination, love.

Singing/silence

Female voice 5:

On my knees –
doing something at once symbolic and down-to-earth,
about responsibility, respect
and remembering;
about life and death, ends and beginnings.
A representative person
who is also a human being
in a particular time and place:
frail, fallible, gifted
with intuition, imagination, love.

Singing/silence

Male voice 5:

On my knees,
in this garden of peace,
I sigh, I groan,
deserted and alone.
I sweat, I ache, I know
these final steps will take my all,
will take much more …

Dear God, Source of my life,
I do this for you, with you
and your intuition, imagination, love.

Singing/silence

Female voice 6:

On my knees –
when I'm down here
actions speak louder than words.
But so low (grassroots, shop floor, street level)
you cannot hear my voice;
and when you put me on a pedestal
you cannot see my face.
If we meet somewhere in the middle,
on common ground,
we can serve each other
and rise together –
sharing intuition, imagination, love.

Singing/silence

Leader sounds the singing bowl.

Leader: Luke 22:39–41 (NRSV)

He came out and went, as was his custom, to the Mount of Olives; and the disciples followed him. When he reached the place, he said to them, 'Pray that you may not come into the time of trial.' Then he withdrew from them about a stone's throw, knelt down, and prayed …

Leader kneels down by the centre table, while other leaders clear the table and extinguish the candles.

Song: 'Stay with me' (Taizé)

People are invited to stay as long as they want/need to.

1 *The Esther Project was an alternative church/fresh expression project of the Uniting Church in Australia. In time, it became an alternative worship community, whose gatherings were formed around deep encounter with the Sacred Story, silence, interactive stations, and/or conversation.*

Sources:

Passages from NRSV copyright 1989, Division of Christian Education of the National Council of the Churches of Christ in the United States of America. Used by permission.

'Woman with ointment', by Jan Sutch Pickard, from *Out of Iona: Words from a Crossroads of the World, Wild Goose Publications*, 2006. Used with permission of Jan Sutch Pickard.

'Jesus anointed, anointing', by Sarah Agnew, first published in *On Wisdom's Wings*, Ginninderra Press, 2013. Used with permission of Sarah Agnew.

Seven actions

A service of prayer & Holy Communion for Maundy Thursday

Stephen J Maunder

This reflective service for Maundy Thursday was first used to provide a new alternative to a Tenebrae liturgy. It includes prayers and meditations, and leads into Holy Communion. The liturgy focuses upon the account of the Last Supper in John 13. Seven candles are lit during the service in response to seven actions, which are noted during the narrative. The lit candles offer a reminder of the presence of light even in the darkness of the eve of Good Friday.

Opening prayer:

Leader: Let us pray together ...

All: God of light and truth,
grant us peace as we gather tonight.
May we draw closer to you as we recall again
the service and suffering of Christ,
in whose name we meet and pray.
Amen

Opening song/hymn

Prayer:

God of grace and truth,
as we move from the brightness of the day's light
to the enfolding darkness of the night-time,
help us to know your light in our hearts,
that in our need for forgiveness and strength
your gracious word may be known.
And then help us to go from this place
renewed in spirit.
In the name of Christ we pray.
Amen

Prayer of confession and assurance:

Lord Christ, in the evening of this day,
forgive us for our lack of attention to you,
our absence of word and action in following you,
and our denial of your place within our lives …

Silence for personal confession

Help us to know your Spirit with us,
your gracious forgiveness,
and your strength in our hearts,
That we may more closely follow you.
Amen

Hymn/song or psalm

Introduction to the Gospel reading (John 13) and candle-lighting:

This evening we shall hear part of John's account of the last evening that Jesus spent with his friends before his arrest. Chapter 13 speaks of actions taken, and decisions made. Some were inspired by goodness, and others not. As the words are read we consider where our place might be within the narrative, and we renew our hope, which is in Christ the light of the world, that through him we might come closer to God.

Action 1 – washing, John 13:1–5:

Now before the festival of the Passover, Jesus knew that his hour had come to depart from this world and go to the Father. Having loved his own who were in the world, he loved them to the end. The devil had already put it into the heart of Judas son of Simon Iscariot to betray him. And during supper Jesus, knowing that the Father had given all things into his hands, and that he had come from God and was going to God, got up from the table, took off his outer robe, and tied a towel around himself. Then he poured water into a basin and began to wash the disciples' feet and to wipe them with the towel that was tied around him.

Let us pray:

Tonight, O God, we recall that your Son arose from the table
to descend to the floor.
We rejoice that in his humility
he left the things of heaven
for the dirt and dust of this world.
Give us humility, we pray,
that we might discover and follow Christ's way and not our own.
Lord, hear us.
Lord, fill us with your truth.

The first candle is lit, followed by pause for reflection ...

Action 2 – cleansing, John 13:6–11:

He came to Simon Peter, who said to him, 'Lord, are you going to wash my feet?' Jesus answered, 'You do not know now what I am doing, but later you will understand.' Peter said to him, 'You will never wash my feet.' Jesus answered, 'Unless I wash you, you have no share with me.' Simon Peter said to him, 'Lord, not my feet only but also my hands and my head!' Jesus said to him, 'One who has bathed does not need to wash, except for the feet, but is entirely clean. And you are clean, though not all of you.' For he knew who was to betray him; for this reason he said, 'Not all of you are clean.'

Meditation:

Feet are not everyone's cup of tea! To take water and wash the feet of the old, the sick, the poor, to take that intimate step of closeness, and to do so in a matter-of-fact way, is a marked act of service.

And to have one's own feet washed can be accompanied by a painful sense of lost independence, as another does for you what you cannot do for yourself. Again and again we become clean through water and through forgiveness. But again and again the cleansing grace of God finds its challenge through our words and actions, our lack of words and lack of action. And then, once again, we need that cleansing grace.

Christ comes and kneels and cleanses us that we might be whole. 'Unless I wash you, you have no part of me,' Jesus says to Peter, and Jesus says that to you and me as well.

Let us pray:

Lord God, help us to accept love when it is shown,
and your love as it is shown through Christ.
Lord, hear us.
Lord, cleanse us through your grace.

The second candle is lit, followed by pause for reflection …

Action 3 – serving, John 13:12–17:

After he had washed their feet, had put on his robe, and had returned to the table, he said to them, 'Do you know what I have done to you? You call me Teacher and Lord – and you are right, for that is what I am. So if I, your Lord and Teacher, have washed your feet, you also ought to wash one another's feet. For I have set you an example, that you also should do as I have done to you. Very truly, I tell you, servants are not greater than their master, nor are messengers greater than the one who sent them. If you know these things, you are blessed if you do them.'

Meditation:

To sort out the seating plan for a wedding can be a nightmare. Who might be offended by not being included on the top table? Who should be seated near that table? Who wouldn't mind sitting with the children? Our egos can be massaged by the importance placed upon us. Jesus lowered himself to the floor and spoke about servants and messengers being no greater than the master … and yet the one whom we serve came to serve. 'Do you know what I have done for you?' Jesus asks. Well, do we? 'If you know these things, you will be blessed if you do them,' says Jesus.

This night we recall the blessedness of following Christ. The blessedness not of a throne or palace. Not a promise of ease. Not a satin cloak. But a towel and a basin, and a crown of thorns and a cross. A way of blessed service here and now, and the promise of peace to come.

Let us pray:

Gracious God, teach us how to serve as we are served.
Lord, hear us.
Lord, fill us with your humble love.

The third candle is lit, followed by pause for reflection …

Action 4 – betraying, John 13:18–30:

'I am not speaking of all of you; I know whom I have chosen. But it is to fulfil the scripture, "The one who ate my bread has lifted his heel against me." I tell you this now, before it occurs, so that when it does occur, you may believe that I am he. Very truly, I tell you, whoever receives one whom I send receives me; and whoever receives me receives him who sent me.'

After saying this Jesus was troubled in spirit, and declared, 'Very truly, I tell you, one of you will betray me.' The disciples looked at one another, uncertain of whom he was speaking. One of his disciples – the one whom Jesus loved – was reclining next to him; Simon Peter therefore motioned to him to ask Jesus of whom he was speaking. So while reclining next to Jesus, he asked him, 'Lord, who is it?' Jesus answered, 'It is the one to whom I give this piece of bread when I have dipped it in the dish.' So when he had dipped the piece of bread, he gave it to Judas son of Simon Iscariot. After he received the piece of bread, Satan entered into him. Jesus said to him, 'Do quickly what you are going to do.' Now no one at the table knew why he said this to him. Some thought that, because Judas had the common purse, Jesus was telling him, 'Buy what we need for the festival'; or, that he should give something to the poor. So, after receiving the piece of bread, he immediately went out. And it was night.

Let us pray:

Loving God, we pray for those who are persecuted
and betrayed for their faith.
Lord, hear us.
Lord, fill us with your strength.

The fourth candle is lit, followed by pause for reflection …

Action 5 – leaving, John 13:31–33:

When he had gone out, Jesus said, 'Now the Son of Man has been glorified, and God has been glorified in him. If God has been glorified in him, God will also glorify him in himself and will glorify him at once. Little children, I am with you only a little longer. You will look for me; and as I said to the Jews so now I say to you, 'Where I am going, you cannot come.'

Let us pray:

Jesus told his disciples that he was going to prepare a place for them.

In silence we remember those who have gone before us,
who have brought the Gospel to us,
who have served Christ amongst us,
and who now are in that place prepared also for us.

Silence

Lord, hear us.
Lord, fill us with your hope.

The fifth candle is lit, followed by pause for reflection …

Action 6 – loving, John 13:34–35:

'I give you a new commandment, that you love one another. Just as I have loved you, you also should love one another. By this everyone will know that you are my disciples, if you have love for one another.'

Let us pray:

Jesus commanded his disciples to love,
even as he knew that betrayal and denial were close at hand.

We pray for those who are rejected and unloved …

We pray for those who are betrayed by those whom they love …

We pray for those who deny their faith through fear …

We pray for those who this night, and every night, fear for their lives …

We pray for those for whom this night will be their last …

Lord, hear us.
Lord, fill us with your compassionate love.

The sixth candle is lit, followed by pause for reflection …

Action 7 – denying, John 13:36–38:

Simon Peter said to him, 'Lord, where are you going?' Jesus answered, 'Where I am going, you cannot follow me now; but you will follow afterward.' Peter said to him, 'Lord, why can I not follow you now? I will lay down my life for you.' Jesus answered, 'Will you lay down your life for me? Very truly, I tell you, before the cock crows, you will have denied me three times.'

Meditation:

The owner was speaking to the man in the chair as he cut his hair. There were strangers in the street, he said. There was a different accent to their voice. A different manner to their dress. It was like being in a foreign land. The waiting customer nodded with a smile and said nothing.

She was with her friends, and the joke she retold was one heard earlier in the day. It was mild in comparison to some, but not so to those who knew the pain of disability or the rejection of difference. The girls laughed, and her closest friend smiled quietly, but said nothing.

He was on his way home after an early appointment, and the driver laughed as he passed the congregation leaving the synagogue. 'Look at them!' he said. His passenger, visible in the mirror, turned away to look out the side window, but said nothing.

Let us pray:

O God, you know that it is often easier and safer
for us to remain silent when we might challenge.
To speak with quiet voices when they need to be louder.
Help us, we pray; re-call us to your service
as Christ re-called your servant Peter by the lakeside,
that we may be fed … and then feed others.

Lord, hear us.
Lord, fill us with your courage, your love and your humility.
Help us in the night-time shadows of fear
to know the continuing light of your presence,
that we may be seen and heard as your people.
Amen

The seventh candle is lit, followed by pause for reflection …

A hymn/song may be sung as the gifts are received and the bread and wine prepared.

Holy Communion:

May you know that the Lord is with you.
And also with you.

May you open your heart to him this night.
May you know his love within you.

Even in the foreboding presence of darkness
May his light shine forth.

In the beginning, before betrayal and denial, O God,
creator of all that is seen and not seen,
you blessed us with the gift of this universe
and this world in which we live.
A place of beauty and challenge,
a place of endless sky and minute form,
a place of similarity and difference.
Present from the beginning was the Word,
bringing forth your grace through the waters of sea and sky,
river and stream, and through all living things.
You formed us in your image,
but rather than praising your name for all that was and is,
again and again we turned away from you,
preferring our own gods and our own ways.

In patience and love, you gave to us those
who called us back to your paths, but we chose different roads.
In a moment of time, you gave the word present before time,
to become flesh and make his home amongst us.
He taught of wholeness and celebration;
he healed those who came to him;
he sought those who had wandered from your way.
But still your grace-filled word was denied.

On this night we recall that after supper Jesus Christ,
the word of love and goodness amongst us,
was arrested and tried,
and that on the day that followed he was crucified.
In remembrance of all that has been done for us,
through the word of creation,

and the word of prophecy,
and the word of all-giving grace,
we join with voices around us and beyond us
in the song of everlasting praise:

Holy, holy, holy Lord, God of power and might,
heaven and earth are full of your glory.
Hosanna in the highest.
Blessed is he who comes in the name of the Lord.
Hosanna in the highest.

On this night Christ our Lord gathered with his friends.
He washed their feet, offered cleansing for their hearts,
and taught them to love as he loved and would love.
Whilst they were eating, he took bread,
and when he had given thanks,
he broke it and gave it to his disciples, saying,
'Take it; this is my body.'
Then he took a cup, and when he had given thanks,
he gave it to them. He told them:
'This is my blood of the covenant, which is poured out for many.
Truly I tell you, I will not drink again from the fruit of the vine
until that day when I drink it new in the kingdom of God.'

Here in this moment of time and in this place,
Christ is present with us as we share bread and wine.
Therefore, O God, pour out your Holy Spirit upon us
and upon these gifts,
that they may be the body and blood of Christ for us,
that we may be his body in this world.
Amen

Lord's Prayer (together)

Christ invites us to share in bread and wine.
Christ invites us to share in service and humility.

Christ invites us to share in strength and renewal.
We gather in faith.

Bread and wine are shared …

Prayer after Communion:

Let us pray:

We give you thanks and praise, O God,
that even in the darkness of this night,
your light shines.
We rejoice that we have shared with Christ
around his table,
and we pray for his strength as we continue to be his body
in this world.
Amen

Final hymn/song

Closing words: Mark 14:32–34:

They went to a place called Gethsemane; and he said to his disciples, 'Sit here while I pray.' He took with him Peter and James and John, and began to be distressed and agitated. And he said to them, 'I am deeply grieved, even to death; remain here, and keep awake.'

There is no final blessing tonight, as the events continue into tomorrow and then to Easter morning resurrection.

The candles remain lit as a sign of hope, as we depart quietly into the night.

Source:

Seven moments

A service of prayer and reflection for Good Friday

Stephen J Maunder

Seven candles are lit in preparation for the service.

Gathering words:

Along this way
We have walked with Christ.

Along this way
We have shared his table.

Along this way
He has washed our feet.

Along this way
We approach the cross.

Along this way
We fear the path.

Behold the lamb of God who takes away the sins of the world.

Opening hymn

Introduction and prayer:

On this day we recall the death of our Lord Jesus Christ. As we hear John's account, we focus on seven moments during that day and, as darkness still seeks to conquer the light, pause to reflect on our own sin, and that of the world.

At the end of each reading we will keep silence as a candle is extinguished to mark the prevailing darkness of this day.

Let us pray:

God of the daytime and the night-time,
God of light and darkness,
God of joy and sorrow,
we worship you.

Through you alone are we able to know that
even in the darkest hours
hope is present through Jesus Christ,
our Saviour.
Amen

1st moment: 'Ecce homo'

Then Pilate took Jesus and had him flogged. And the soldiers wove a crown of thorns and put it on his head, and they dressed him in a purple robe. They kept coming up to him, saying, 'Hail, King of the Jews!' and striking him on the face. Pilate went out again and said to them, 'Look, I am bringing him out to you to let you know that I find no case against him.' So Jesus came out, wearing the crown of thorns and the purple robe. Pilate said to them, 'Here is the man!' When the chief priests and the police saw him, they shouted, 'Crucify him! Crucify him!' Pilate said to them, 'Take him yourselves and crucify him; I find no case against him.' The Jews answered him, 'We have a law, and according to that law he ought to die because he has claimed to be the Son of God.'

John 19:1–7 (NRSV)

We pray:

Lord, have mercy,
Christ, have mercy,
Lord, have mercy.

The 1st candle is extinguished.

Silence

Reflection:

'Here is the man', 'Ecce homo', the Roman prefect said as he offered Jesus to the crowd. No name now for this nuisance-man whose silent threat causes such alarm. Yet even the no-name 'Ecce homo' has become a title for paintings, sculptures and verse over the centuries. A no-name title becoming his title, and a no-name handing-over soon to become his fate. Ecce homo – the Word made flesh.

2nd moment: Gabbatha

Now when Pilate heard this, he was more afraid than ever. He entered his headquarters again and asked Jesus, 'Where are you from?' But Jesus gave him no answer. Pilate therefore said to him, 'Do you refuse to speak to me? Do you not know that I have power to release you, and power to crucify you?' Jesus answered him, 'You would have no power over me unless it had been given you from above; therefore the one who handed me over to you is guilty of a greater sin.' From then on Pilate tried to release him, but the Jews cried out, 'If you release this man, you are no friend of the emperor. Everyone who claims to be a king sets himself against the emperor.'

When Pilate heard these words, he brought Jesus outside and sat on the judge's bench at a place called the Stone Pavement, or in Hebrew Gabbatha. Now it was the day of Preparation for the Passover; and it was about noon. He said to the Jews, 'Here is your King!' They cried out, 'Away with him! Away with him! Crucify him!' Pilate asked them, 'Shall I crucify your King?' The chief priests answered, 'We have no king but the emperor.' Then he handed him over to them to be crucified.

John 19:8–16a (NRSV)

We pray:

Lord, have mercy,
Christ, have mercy,
Lord, have mercy.

The 2nd candle is extinguished.

Silence

A hymn may be sung.

3rd moment: Golgotha

So they took Jesus; and carrying the cross by himself, he went out to what is called The Place of the Skull, which in Hebrew is called Golgotha. There they crucified him, and with him two others, one on either side, with Jesus between them. Pilate also had an inscription written and put on the cross.

It read, 'Jesus of Nazareth, the King of the Jews.' Many of the Jews read this inscription, because the place where Jesus was crucified was near the city; and it was written in Hebrew, in Latin, and in Greek. Then the chief priests of the Jews said to Pilate, 'Do not write, "The King of the Jews", but, "This man said, I am King of the Jews."' Pilate answered, 'What I have written I have written.'

John 19:16b–22 (NRSV)

We pray:

Lord, have mercy,
Christ, have mercy,
Lord, have mercy.

The 3rd candle is extinguished.

Silence

Meditation:

The article was finished and passed on to the editor for approval. Within a few minutes the call came. 'Are you *sure* you want to say this?' she asked.

'It's what happened,' the reporter replied. 'Those were the words that were used.'

'But they don't quite reflect our brand, fit in with our readers. Maybe you could say "it seemed" … or "it appeared that" … or "she was unclear".'

'But she wasn't. She was clear about what was said and when it occurred and what was meant by it – very clear.'

'OK,' the editor responded, 'if it goes wrong, I'll take the flak. Let it be as you have written.'

Pilate, in a moment of bravery, insists on what has been written – no fudging – 'the King of the Jews' it is. Even in the face of the crowd, sometimes it has to be said as it is. Even when the mood of the crowd threatens, sometimes it needs to be said as it is.

A hymn may be sung.

4th moment: Casting lots

When the soldiers had crucified Jesus, they took his clothes and divided them into four parts, one for each soldier. They also took his tunic; now the tunic was seamless, woven in one piece from the top. So they said to one another, 'Let us not tear it, but cast lots for it to see who will get it.' This was to fulfil what the scripture says, 'They divided my clothes among themselves, and for my clothing they cast lots.'

And that is what the soldiers did.

John 19:23–25 (NRSV)

We pray:

Lord, have mercy,
Christ, have mercy,
Lord, have mercy.

The 4th candle is extinguished.

Silence

5th moment: 'Here is your mother'

Meanwhile, standing near the cross of Jesus were his mother, and his mother's sister, Mary the wife of Clopas, and Mary Magdalene. When Jesus saw his mother and the disciple whom he loved standing beside her, he said to his mother, 'Woman, here is your son.' Then he said to the disciple, 'Here is your mother.' And from that hour the disciple took her into his own home.

John 19:25–27 (NRSV)

We pray:

Lord, have mercy,
Christ, have mercy,
Lord, have mercy.

The 5th candle is extinguished.

Silence

Reflection:

In a moment all can change.
That moment of fearful angelic promise.
That moment of Bethlehem's birth pain and first-nursing.
That moment of fleeing.
That moment of apparent rejection.
That moment …
So many moments with him.
And now this moment,
this handing over,
as the care given to him from birth to death
is now received from him,
and in this moment,
a new home for him and for me.

6th moment: Finished

After this, when Jesus knew that all was now finished, he said (in order to fulfil the scripture), 'I am thirsty.' A jar full of sour wine was standing there. So they put a sponge full of the wine on a branch of hyssop and held it to his mouth. When Jesus had received the wine, he said, 'It is finished.' Then he bowed his head and gave up his spirit.

John 19:28–30 (NRSV)

We pray:

Lord, have mercy,
Christ, have mercy,
Lord, have mercy.

The 6th candle is extinguished.

Silence

Reflection:

Finished.
So final a word,
but what is ever really finished,
accomplished,
completed,
except life itself?

A race run,
a record set,
only serves to herald
the next attempt,
a new champion
and holder of the prize.

But once for all
a death of life,
an obscuring of light
bringing
darkness in its wake,
as a moment of completion
is echoed with finality.
Finished ...
the end ...
extinguished light ...
... but only till a brighter dawn.

A hymn may be sung.

7th moment: Pierced

Since it was the day of Preparation, the Jews did not want the bodies left on the cross during the sabbath, especially because that sabbath was a day of great solemnity. So they asked Pilate to have the legs of the crucified men broken and the bodies removed. Then the soldiers came and broke the legs of the first and of the other who had been crucified with him. But when they came to Jesus and saw that he was already dead, they did not break his legs. Instead, one of the soldiers pierced his side with a spear, and at once blood and water came out.

John 19:31–34 (NRSV)

We pray:

Lord, have mercy,
Christ, have mercy,
Lord, have mercy.
Amen

The 7th candle is extinguished.

Silence

Reflection:

Seven moments of the ordinary.

Crowds,
fear,
power.
Inhumanity made ordinary …

And so it continues as those with power
quash unrest,
break limbs,
execute trouble-makers,
instil fear.

As the chilling ordinariness of shoes and spectacles piled high whilst those who had chosen and bought them, cleaned them and worn them, are nameless numbers in a place of everyday death. No-names, each loved by God, but treated as less than human by others who, being loved by God themselves, risk their very humanity.

And we pause. And we wonder.

In seven moments of ordinary violence, would we be different?
Other days will soon come …

the deep, deep sorrow of a garden visit met with a name;
a fear-filled room gathering an unexpected visitor;
a sad path home becoming a way back to hope;
a picnic transformed into a place of restitution.
But for now the candles are extinguished,
and the darkness prevails.

Prayers:

Let us pray.

We pray for those for whom the terrifying has become the ordinary:
for victims of warfare;
for children and mothers unable to live in homes that are their own;
for fighters who have become immune to the cries of others;
and for politicians who hear only praise.

Silence

Lord of the cross,
Hear our prayer.

We pray for ourselves, if we have become immune to those who suffer,
who have no name, who count for little.
We ask for forgiveness for those times when we failed to speak or act.

Silence

Lord of the cross,
Hear our prayer.

We give thanks for those who remind us that
even in the shadows of pain
humanity may shine forth.
We give thanks for those who care for the dead and the dying,
for those who bring hope.

Silence

Lord of the cross,
Hear our prayer.

Lord of the cross,
in you alone do we find our hope,
even when hope is gone.
Amen

Final hymn

A closing reading:

After these things, Joseph of Arimathea, who was a disciple of Jesus, though a secret one because of his fear of the Jews, asked Pilate to let him take away the body of Jesus. Pilate gave him permission; so he came and removed his body. Nicodemus, who had at first come to Jesus by night, also came, bringing a mixture of myrrh and aloes, weighing about a hundred pounds. They took the body of Jesus and wrapped it with the spices in linen cloths, according to the burial custom of the Jews. Now there was a garden in the place where he was crucified, and in the garden there was a new tomb in which no one had ever been laid. And so, because it was the Jewish day of Preparation, and the tomb was nearby, they laid Jesus there.

John 19:38–42 (NRSV)

Final prayer and departure:

When hope has left
Still we watch and wait.

When darkness prevails
Still we search for light.

When the road is hidden
Still we seek a guide.

Christ of the cross,
hold us in these moments
as we wait for a garden vision,
a mealtime revelation,
a locked-room blessing,
and a lakeside renewal.
We go in peace.

Folk depart quietly.

Source:

Pentecost is now

A short act of worship

Joy Mead

Suggested song: 'Wind of change', by Fred Kaan, from *The Only Earth We Know*, Hope Publishing; suggested tune 'Au clair de la lune'

Bible reading:

When the day of Pentecost had come, they were all together in one place. And suddenly from heaven there came a sound like the rush of a violent wind, and it filled the entire house where they were sitting. Divided tongues, as of fire, appeared among them, and a tongue rested on each of them. All of them were filled with the Holy Spirit and began to speak in other languages, as the Spirit gave them ability.

Acts 2:1–4 (NRSV)

Growing hope (a reflection):

Whichever way we look at the symbolism in this story, it is about a mind-blowing, heart-searching moment. The wind of change challenges and disturbs not only individuals but whole communities. Martin Luther King spoke of the storm which will not abate until a just distribution of the fruits of the earth enables all people to live dignified and decent lives. Spirituality does not exist apart from the social context. Look at when and where the story in Acts is set. The Spirit coming is about more than individual inwardness. It means engagement: what you do with the material part of your life; how you connect with other people, how you relate to other living things, how you walk on the earth.

Pentecost isn't a once and for all happening but ongoing and energising hope here, now, in this world, in this place. It's about that which sustains us, enables us, provokes a just anger and arouses compassion. It's about spirit-filled life bursting out of encounter with darkness and suffering and it's characterised by joy – not the shallow cheeriness of jolly Christians but the deep joy of those who hope and hear the lark's song in the storm.

Prayer:

Living Spirit
help us to hold on to our Pentecost moments
as we walk into the storm.

May we know the value of story, dream and poetry
that tell us of mystery and wonder, joy and pain,
hopes and visions.

May we see that narrow horizons limit compassion
and abstractions blanket feelings.

May we not be afraid
to imagine life as it is meant to be
for all people;
to live as if the world we long for
were already here.

Living Spirit
help us to hold on to our Pentecost moments
as we walk into the storm.

May we have the vision to see
understanding as different from knowledge,
that money is not necessarily the answer
and the rich do not always do things better
than everyone else.

Living Spirit
help us to hold on to our Pentecost moments
as we walk into the storm.

May we long for that understanding of prosperity
that is about sharing the good things of life
and realise that growth must be emotional and moral.
Economic growth is no longer an option.

Living Spirit
help us to hold on to our Pentecost moments
as we walk into the storm.

Lead us to ways that hallow all life
and honour compassion and kindness,
ways that ask questions about what we value
and do not dismiss the people's dreams
because they are illogical,
can't pay for themselves,
get in the way of the economic machine
or disturb the slavish devotion to the laws
of supply and demand.

Living Spirit
help us to hold on to our Pentecost moments
as we walk into the storm.

May we understand what repentance means:
that it is more than restructuring our lives.
May we appreciate that lament
is part of living, a place to express that depth of sorrow
out of which hope will come.

Give us a spirituality of resistance and struggle
that refuses to let injustice have the last word.

Living Spirit
help us to hold on to our Pentecost moments
as we walk into the storm.

—

End worship with the lighting of a candle and silence …

Draw us into the dance

A liturgy for Trinity Sunday

Thom M Shuman

Call to worship:

Called to be faithful stewards of creation, we come to worship:
To sing to the One
who has created all that is good, beautiful and true,
and who has shared everything with us.

Called to be disciples of Jesus Christ, we come to learn:
To follow the One
who meets us in every moment of our lives,
in every place we find ourselves.

Called to proclaim the Good News of Easter, we come to find the words:
To be taught by the Spirit,
who moves in and through us
as we serve the world.

Prayer:

Hearing your whisper,
creation tingles with anticipation,
knowing that goodness and wonder
are your heart's desires.

Listening to your instructions,
the universe shimmers with delight,
and all creatures fall down
and worship you.

Imaginative God,
you are as close
as the early-morning breeze.
You spoke,
and ran forth
to sprinkle the heavens
with shimmering stars;
you poured the waters of grace
into the hollows of the earth
so that all life might emerge.

Bone of our bone,
flesh of our flesh,
you are as close
as the love which
fills our hearts.

You dreamed,
and flowed over chaos –
shaping, spinning, weaving
peace, wonder and joy
into the fabric of all life.
Your passion for hope
became flames which
dance in our hearts.

Spirit of fanciful faith,
you are as close
as a butterfly's wings
brushing our cheeks.

You are closer to us
than we ever dared hope,
God in Community, Holy and One,
and so we lift our prayers to you, saying …

The Lord's Prayer

Song

Call to reconciliation:

When God looks at us,
the One who created us sees hope, joy, grace, life.
But all too often,
others see us as broken, hurtful, sinful …
Let us confess our deeds and words to the One who loves us
and longs to re-create us in the image of true life.

Prayer for forgiveness:

Why do you pay us any attention,
Artist of creation?
Created in your image,
we show faces filled with desire to do good,
but offer hearts filled with anger to those around us.

Called to be disciples of Christ,
we all too often are seen chasing after
the false promises of the easy life.

Offered the role of being stewards of creation,
we think that everything you have created is to be used up
so we can enjoy life,
giving no thought for future generations.

Yet you have declared everything you created to be good,
even us, God of unexpected grace.
So we know that,
in Christ Jesus, our Lord and Saviour,
you will reshape our greed into generosity,
our bitterness into blessings
and our brokenness into lives
poured out in service to our sisters and brothers.

Silence

Assurance of pardon:

Lives that are chaotic become cradles of peace;
hearts malformed by meanness are reshaped into goodness;
souls filled with despair are cleansed with grace.
This is the good news:
the God who created us
is the same God who redeems us.

The God who redeems us
is the God who sends us forth to serve.
Thanks be to God, we are forgiven!
Amen

Prayer of dedication/Offering

Use our gifts, Holy Community of Love,
as you reach out to heal the broken,
as you take the hands of the lost
and as you pull out a chair to welcome
the outcast to your table
of wonder and hope.
This we pray.
Amen

Bible readings: Genesis 1:1–2:4a, Psalm 8, Matthew 28:16–20, 2 Corinthians 13:11–13

Song

Reflection:

I toss
God
into the air,
watching the divine
spin and sparkle;

next I add
Jesus
to the mix, carefully
throwing each
from one hand

to the
other, confident
I will not drop either
One;

then, pulling the
Spirit
from my back pocket, I begin
that simply
complex
process of keeping all
Three
in the air;

as I settle
into the rhythm
of keeping the
Holy Community
under my control
(propelling them
faster and faster
until they
become a
blur no one can
comprehend),

the audience sits
spellbound
by my theological
dexterity,
and none of us
hear
your gentle whisper,

*'Why do you think
it is all an act?'*

Or:

There are all sorts of explanations that might be offered when it comes to the doctrine of the Trinity, all kinds of theologians can be quoted, all manner of creeds and confessions might be affirmed. And – after all that – most of us are *still* confused.

One image I find helpful is that of the dance – the Holy Community joining hands and joyfully being in relationship with one another. Sometimes, God is the one who keeps the underlying beat going, Jesus might teach a new step that the others had not thought of yet and the Spirit will improvise the tune so that the tempo and rhythm is not always the same. But they are always in step; they are always focusing on one another, even as each is aware of the particular part they play in the dance.

And they want to share that dance with us – to teach us the steps, to help us hear the music.

The Father reaches out in Love, inviting us to dance, to show us those moves called grace, wonder, laughter, peace. The Son connects with us in Love, taking us by the hand to draw us into the dance, whether we are hurting, or angry, or grieving, or broken, or lost. And the Spirit welcomes us, enfolding us in Love, as we are taught to dance with abandon, with kindness, with hope, with gentleness.

And as we dance, we discover that the Trinity is not so much a doctrine as it is a relationship – with us!

Song

Great prayer of thanksgiving:

May God in Community be with you.
And with you as well.

Shaped in the divine image, let us open ourselves to the Creator.
With grace-filled hearts, we come to the Redeemer's table.

Called to be God's household, let us offer our praises.

We rejoice that the Holy Spirit has brought us,
from many places,
here to our home.

At the beginning,
God of Imagination,
you finger-painted
sunrises and sunsets
on the blank canvas of chaos.
You sang creation's cantata,
while suns, moons and stars
kept watch over your delights.

You laughed, while
lions, tigers and bears
danced joyfully in the meadows,
and everything that
wiggles, creeps, crawls
clapped their hands in time.

When you would have
clothed us in glory,
we found sin and death
to be a more comfortable fit.

Prophets came teaching obedience
and calling us to faithful lives,
but we continued to insist
on having control of our souls.

So, you sent Jesus
to make our brokenness
whole once again.
So, with grace, love and unity,
our faithful companions and teachers,
and with all the saints of every time and place,
we lift our songs of thanksgiving:

How majestic is your name in all the earth, Holy One.
All creation greets you with glad songs of praise.
Hosanna in the highest!

Blessed is the One who comes to make us disciples.
Hosanna in the highest!

Holy are you, God-over-us,
and blessed is Jesus Christ, God-with-us.
He took off glory's garb
to put on humanity;
he set aside heaven's honour
to be crowned with disgrace;
he spoke of love and hope,
silencing our enemy, pride;
he went into the grave
to free us from death's grasp.

As we remember his life, death and resurrection,
as we celebrate his re-creating power in us,
we speak of that mystery called faith:
Christ died, crowned with death's thorns.
Christ was raised, crowned with resurrection's wonder.
Christ will come, to crown us with glory and honour.

Send your Spirit to flow over
the gifts of the bread and the cup,
and to bring light and goodness
to those who gather around your Table.

As we break the Bread of life,
may we become living hope
to a world mired in despair.

As we drink from the Cup of grace,
may we cradle your kindness and peace
in our hearts and souls,
so we might be poured out
to those who thirst for your
peace and gentleness.

And when your dreams which began at creation
are realised and all time comes to an end –
when we gather around your Table

with saints and sinners, disciples and deniers –
we will find ourselves closer to you
than we ever thought possible,
singing your praises forever and ever,
God in Community, Holy and One.
Amen

Prayers of concern

Communion

Song

Sending and benediction:

God, who created you in the divine image, sends you forth:
**We go: to reflect the presence of our Creator
to everyone we meet along the way.**

Jesus, who has redeemed you,
has established God's Kingdom in our midst:
**We go: to bring healing and hope
to all the broken of the world.**

The Holy Spirit, who calls you to be God's people,
goes with you to many places:
**We go: to tear down the walls which divide us,
and to build lives of trust for all God's children.**

And now,
may the peace of the rolling waves,
the peace of the silent mountains,
the peace of the singing stars,
and the deep, deep peace of the Prince of Peace
be with you now and forever.
Amen

As you come and go

Readings, prayers and poems for World Oceans Day (June 8th)

Tom Gordon

The ocean

This piece would work well with two voices.

I watch you, friendly ocean,
as I walk beside your edge.
I watch you, friendly ocean,
as you caress my toes
with gentle touch.
I watch you, friendly ocean,
as you say 'Hi!' in your coming
and 'So long!' in your going,
again, and again, and again.
I watch you, friendly ocean,
as I welcome you home to my shore.

But do I know you, mysterious ocean,
as I walk along my fringe of sand?
Do I know you, mysterious ocean,
as you come, differently now
than you've been before?
Do I know you, mysterious ocean?
And do you know me in your arriving
and in your departing?
And do you care?
Do I know you, mysterious ocean,
as your world touches mine once more?

I fear you, raging ocean,
as you crash upon my world.
I fear you, raging ocean,
as you batter my once secure boundaries
with unconstrained supremacy.
I fear you, raging ocean,
as you come, uninvited,
uncontrolled, unrepressed,
gatecrasher on my peaceful habitation.
I fear you, raging ocean,
for I know your destructiveness has returned.

But do I understand you, troubled ocean,
even in your hysterical rage?
Do I understand you, troubled ocean,
as I might understand my own fears,
born out of humanity's restlessness?
Do I understand you, troubled ocean,
in your need to invade,
your driven, natural passion
to come and threaten me, angry as you are?
Do I understand you, troubled ocean;
and does it bother you if I don't?

I can use you, wonderful ocean,
to cruise your surface as I choose.
I can use you, wonderful ocean,
for my leisure, and my commerce,
and my travel plans.
I can use you, wonderful ocean,
to garner your harvest
and marvel at your sights and wonders,
your beauty and your life.
I can use you, wonderful ocean,
because you are mine.

But can I control you, terrible ocean,
as I gaze upon your depths?
Can I control you, terrible ocean,
and shackle your power,
or manacle your strength?
Can I control you, terrible ocean,
and build cities upon your surface,
and expand my empires,
and stretch my influence beyond these shores?
Can I control you, terrible ocean,
and bend you to my will alone?

I need you, brother ocean,
so that you and I can live in harmony.
I need you, sister ocean,

as you welcome me
into your tender, warm, inviting arms.
I need you, mother ocean,
to be the birth of my life,
the sustainer of my being,
the enabler of my future.
I need you, father ocean,
to be strong and permanent for me.

But can I love you, brother ocean,
and walk with you as an equal?
Can I love you, sister ocean,
and believe you when you say,
'Come, and rest with me'?
Can I love you, mother ocean,
or will I have no regard for your nurture
as I turn my back on you
and walk away?
Can I love you, father ocean,
or am I the strong one now?

Saying sorry to the oceans

This piece might follow a reading concerning the effects of pollution and global warming on the world's oceans and sea life. It would work well with two voices.

You touch me,
and I ignore you.

God of the ocean's touch,
forgive me for not finding
healing in your gentle hands.

You feed me,
and I give you garbage.

God of the ocean's plenty,
forgive me for taking all your goodness

and offering you only my scraps.

You are patient with me,
and I don't care.

God of the ocean's tolerance,
forgive me for knowing you're always around
and not caring for your welfare.

You nurture me,
and I give you hurt.

God of the ocean's love,
forgive me for taking your acceptance
and replacing it with rejection.

You are constant for me,
and I am fickle.

God of the ocean's constancy,
forgive me for my thoughtlessness
and for not thinking how much you matter.

You return again,
and I take you for granted.

God of the ocean's rhythms,
forgive me for seeing you once again
and for ignoring your presence.

You call out to me,
and I ignore your pleading.

Help me to be still
and listen to the ocean's voice.

You offer me beauty,
and I respond with ugliness.

Help me to open my eyes
and wonder at the ocean's mystery.

You love me,
and I love only myself.

Help me to believe the ocean's promises
and to fall in love with it again.

You embrace me,
and I shrug you off.

Help me to give myself to the ocean's embrace
and be thankful for this gift.

You need me,
and I don't care any more.

Help me to live in partnership with your oceans
and care more than I do.

Amen

Wonder and awe (a reflection)

Not surprisingly, when the writers of the books of the Bible turn to the wonder of God's creation, and offer praise for what they see, the oceans are well-represented.

In the first chapter of Genesis we read:

And God said, 'Let there be a vault between the waters to separate water from water.' So God made the vault and separated the water under the vault from the water above it. And it was so. God called the vault 'sky'. And there was evening, and there was morning – the second day ... And God said, 'Let the water under the sky be gathered to one place, and let dry ground appear.' And it was so. God called the dry ground 'land', and the gathered waters he called 'seas'. And God saw that it was good. (Gen 1:6–10, NIV)

Of course God did! That's what people saw and knew and believed. The oceans were wonderful. They were different from the dry land, just as heaven and earth were different. God had made it so. Isn't God just amazing and worthy of our praise? Why would we not praise such a Creator God?

The Psalmist, taking all of this and putting it into expressions of religious praise, offers us this in Psalm 104:

You set the earth on its foundations, so that it shall never be shaken. You cover it with the deep as with a garment; the waters stood above the mountains. At your rebuke they flee; at the sound of your thunder they take to flight. They rose up to the mountains, ran down to the valleys to the place that you appointed for them. You set a boundary that they may not pass, so that they might not again cover the earth. (Psalm 104:5–9, NRSV)

Such writers look at the world and it speaks to them of God. I marvel at that. I'm amazed by such faith.

But let's stop for a moment and ponder ... When the biblical writers speak this way, are they not using their understanding of God as the ultimate metaphor? The 'God' label is a way of expressing wonder and awe for a wonderful world. I can understand that. I appreciate that. But there are many who cannot, and will not, use the 'God' metaphor. It doesn't work for them. And yet, do they not also live with awe and wonder at what this amazing world contains? There may be different metaphors that work for them – Mother Nature, the natural world and the like – but do they not also have praise in their heart for what they see and know?

At the end of the day, the issue is not what metaphor is used or what label is chosen. All of us – from a God or a Mother Nature perspective – are seeking to do the same thing: we are all seeking to express our response to a remarkable world.

For me, in my life and living, when I look at the wonderful world and have no words to describe it, I simply stand in awe. And when I have no voice, I let the world do the speaking for me.

My voice

I hear the wind; the howl and scream;
the rage and shaking fist that rocks the world.
I hear the wind,
and know the angry gale can speak for me.

I watch the waves; the pounding surf;
the spreading, drenching spray that drowns the shore.
I watch the waves,
and know the angry sea can speak for me.

I feel the rain; the biting shards
that harshly sting my face and drench my dreams.
I feel the rain,
and know the angry storm can speak for me.

I hear the crash of thunder claps
that make me shrink with fear; this unseen power;
these thunder peals …
I know the angry roar can speak for me.

I see the flash of lightning fill the sky;
destructive force of saw-toothed light.
When lightning strikes,
I know its violent surge can speak for me.

Creation's voice, in all its might,
I know could be my voice, when I am voiceless now.
When earth and oceans shout aloud,
I know my world's own voice can speak – and shout – for me.

Pathways (a reflection)

In Exodus chapter 14, the children of Israel, under the leadership of Moses, have been enslaved in Egypt. As they escape, their route to freedom is blocked by the Red Sea, the ocean of their day. There is panic. There is anger. There is bitterness that God has promised them a way to freedom and then snatched it from their grasp. There is distress. Moses expresses all of this to God. And here is God's response:

Bible reading: Exodus 14:26–30

A miraculous deliverance? Or the 'Red Sea' being a mistranslation of 'the Reed Sea', a marshy area that regularly dried up and flooded again, making the 'miraculous' story more believable? God intervening, one way or another, to protect and deliver his chosen people? Who knows?

To be honest, I'm not sure it matters. For me, this whole story is a metaphor for the human condition and our relationship with anything that blocks our onward progress or threatens our journey forward.

And the lesson? Not that if we have 'God on our side' we will always be victorious. But simply the belief – or at least the hope – that no barrier is insurmountable. There is no ocean, no mountain, no threat, no hurdle that cannot be overcome with God's help.

True? I believe it to be so.

Barriers

I once had an argument with my mother.
She said,
'You have to believe God will give you guidance.
God has promised to point the way,
to give you His direction,
to make things obvious.'
So I prayed to God for guidance,
expecting to be shown the way,
to find directions written with His finger on a wall,
with everything clear.

But it wasn't.
So I argued with my mother,
and told her she was wrong.
And then I decided …
It's too easy to let someone else –
even a divine being –
make the decisions for me.
Can't I decide?
Can't I work out the way ahead?
Can't I choose my direction, even when I get it wrong?
Can't I do my best to make things clear?

Maybe that's what my mother really meant.
Maybe I shouldn't have argued ...

I once had an argument with God.
He said,
'If you have faith, you'll have all the guidance you need.
I promise to point the way for you.
All you need to do is follow directions
and things will be fine.'
So I trusted God for guidance.
But there was no way ahead that made any sense.
No magic finger wrote instructions on my wall.
Nothing was clear.

My faith wasn't working.
So I argued with God.
I told God He was wrong.

And then I decided ...
It's too easy to let God –
or even my mother –
give me advice about decisions.
Can't I decide?
Can't I work out the way ahead?
Can't I choose my direction, even when I get it wrong?
Can't I do my best to make things clear?

Maybe that's what God really meant.
Maybe I shouldn't have argued …

Now I have arguments with myself.
Part of me says,
'You'll always have guidance.
You'll find a way;
there will be no barriers to your progress;
the way ahead will be obvious.'
So I looked for guidance,
expecting the oceans to divide,
or at least to know it was possible,
so the way ahead would be clear.
But it wasn't.
So I argued with myself.
I thought I'd got it wrong.
And then I decided …
It's too easy to think everything will be OK
all of the time.
There will always be barriers that appear.
Can't I work out a way past them
or round them
or over them
or through them?

Maybe that's what the parting of the Red Sea actually meant.

Maybe I shouldn't have doubted myself ...

Storms

Bible reading: Mark 4:35–41

Voice 1:

When storms around me rage,
I'll cry in fear.

When waves would threaten me,
I might succumb.

When oceans boil with rage,
I face my doom.
When winds roar and scream and curse,
I breathe my last.
And yet ...

Voice 2:

When storms assail my life,
I will survive.

When waves lift up with power,
I too can rise.

When anger does its worst,
I'll not lose faith.

When winds would tear me down,
I'll not give in.

And so ...

Voice 1:

I'll trust a higher power,
and find my peace.

I'll give myself to grace,
and stillness know.
I'll find an inner strength
that will not fail.

I'll give myself to faith
in tranquil calm.

And then ...

Voice 2:

Though storms will rage again,
I will not fear.

Though waves rise higher still,
I'll not succumb.

Though oceans' anger shouts,
I'll not give up.

Though all this world's disturbed,
I'll find my Peace.

Respect for the sea

Donald was a fisherman. So were his four brothers, and their father. So were his three uncles, two of his brothers-in-law, three nephews, his next-door neighbour, and most of the other men in the village. So had been his grandfather and countless generations before that. And it was no different for almost every other family in the vicinity. Donald was a fisherman, for that's what men did in every village down the coast.

Fishing was the life and livelihood for those who harvested the fruits of the ocean. It was the talk of the pubs. It was the economy of family life. It was the aspiration of the children. It was at the heart of everything. And it was the sustainer of faith, for there was not one family in the village who wasn't represented in one of the many local places of worship – mission halls, Brethren meeting houses, parish churches, Roman Catholic chapels. Sometimes even Donald – foul-mouthed, hard-drinking Donald – went to church, for the fleet never sailed on a Sunday, and no work was done repairing the boats or the nets on the day of rest. And when, on most Sundays, he didn't join the family for worship, he would be with the other men down at the harbour, leaning on the rail, smoking his pipe, and talking about the fishing.

Donald was a lover of the ocean. It provided his livelihood, as it had done for generations. In days gone by it was 'following the herring', 'fishing for the silver darlings' that was the norm. The ocean was a plentiful giver. The ocean was a friend. Even now, when fishing in the Atlantic and the North Sea was the province of super-trawlers and factory ships, and the fishing from Donald's harbour was confined to lobsters, langoustines and crabs, the fishing still mattered and the ocean deeps had to be respected.

Sometimes Donald cursed the oceans, as all the fishermen did. When the tides were wrong; when the weather fronts forced the boats to stay tied up in the harbour; when ferocious squalls blew up unexpectedly and you had to 'run the storm' to get safely home; when the great waves threatened your little boat, Donald could curse with the best of them. But there was always respect. The ocean was a challenging friend. And even in its quietest, most serene moments, the ocean could turn on you.

The young boy who slipped off the harbour wall one wet Sunday morning didn't understand that. He shouldn't have been there in the first place. He should have been in the mission hall with his mother and little sister. And he shouldn't have been stupid enough to be out at the end of the harbour bar, not with such a wind blowing, and the tide turning, and a storm brewing. But he wanted to fish, and the best fishing with his father's old rod was at the narrow entrance to the harbour.

It was Donald's brother who saw the lad slip and sprinted to grab the lifebelt. In an instant, he was in the water, swimming strongly to the struggling boy. Donald was the first to respond to the shouts to get the boat out, and within minutes he and two others were turning their outboard round the end of the harbour wall and facing a running tide.

It wasn't a dramatic rescue. Donald's brother was still in the water when they got to him with the outboard, hanging on to the metal ladder at the end of the harbour wall. The young lad was cradled in the lifebelt and a big fisherman's arm. It only took a few minutes to get a soaking man and an embarrassed teenager back to dry land, and eventually to the warmth and safety of home.

It wasn't a dramatic rescue, though it made the local paper the following week. It's what you do when you're a fisherman and you hear the call and somebody needs you. After all, it was Donald's brother who got wet and did all the hard work. Donald just did what he had to do. But he also had to say what he had to say.

'You have to respect the sea, son,' he said to the young lad. 'It can get you, just like that …'

It was back to the fishing for Donald on the Monday morning. He and the boys on the boat had a good week. On the following Sunday, Donald didn't join the other men down at the harbour, leaning on the rail, smoking their pipes, and talking about the fishing. Donald went to the mission hall with his wife, and he was delighted to see a young teenager there too with his mother and little sister. And Donald hoped no one saw a big fisherman wipe away a tear from his cheek when the pastor announced the final hymn, 'Eternal Father, strong to save', and as a grateful sailor sang in his gruff, fisherman's voice, 'O hear us when we cry to Thee for those in peril on the sea.'

O ocean!

I live close to the ocean, as the waters of the North Sea invade my homeland through the incision of the Firth of Forth on the south-east of Scotland. Not far from my home there is a stretch of sand called the Longniddry bents, where I often walk my dog – at least, I walk as she runs madly up and down the sand and in and out of the waves that are breaking on the shore. I've lost count the number of times I've stood and marvelled at the rhythm of the tide – in and out, coming and going, tense and relaxing, inhaling and exhaling, almost in sync with my own breathing. The vastness of the ocean, right at my feet, is a reminder of the rhythms of life, the constancy of our world, the music of creation, the mystery of time and eternity ...

I wrote this one day when I'd come back from a shoreline walk. I leave it with you as my final thought for World Oceans Day:

O, ocean strong! O, ocean wide!
Your power cannot be brushed aside
by my weak sense of what I know,
my wonder as you come and go.

O, ocean clear! O, ocean calm!
How dare I do you dreadful harm,
and disregard my anguished woes,
as here I watch you come and go?

O, ocean great! O, ocean fine!
I am forever intertwined
with you, whose waves and tides still show
you'll never cease to come and go.

O, ocean vast! O, ocean deep!
Mysterious friend, my shores you sweep,
and tell me what I need to know –
you're always here, to come and go.

O, ocean then! O, ocean now!
We're hand-in-hand – the I and Thou,
eternity's adagio
in time – just as you come and go.

Sources:

'My voice' adapted from 'Creation speaks for me' in *New Journeys Now Begin*, Tom Gordon, Wild Goose Publications, 2006

'Respect for the sea' adapted from 'Andrew' in *A Blessing to Follow*, Tom Gordon, Wild Goose Publications, 2009

Every day is a day of joy

An all-age communion for summertime on the theme of play

Thom M Shuman

Opening responses:

Give thanks to God!
We thank God for the joy of jumping rope
and the laughter in playing leapfrog!

Give thanks to God at all times!
We thank God for the cool waters of a pool
on a hot summer day,
and the way the water surprises us
when we first jump in!

Give thanks to God at all times and for all things!
We thank God for fireflies making our nights brighter
and for butterflies which tickle us awake after a nap!

Prayer:

Every day is a day of wonder,
Imaginative God:
filled with empty cardboard boxes
that can take us to the moon,
and long afternoon games
where the score is never kept.

You rub the sleep from our eyes
so we can see you at play:
in the children on the corner,
in the teenager balancing on a skateboard,
in the older couple waltzing the night away.

From the cereal which crackles us awake
to the cat stalking the sunbeam;
from the baby just discovering her toes
to the old man who secretly puts sacks of tomatoes
on his neighbours' porches;
from the hummingbird drinking nectar
to the dog grabbing the hose out of our hand –

every day is a day of laughter,
Smiling Christ.

We hear the squeals of the children
jumping on the trampoline,
and the sweet sound of a ball
off the bat down at the playground.
We hope no one sees us
as we try out the hopscotch
drawn in chalk on the sidewalk,
and we smile from our window
at the father taking training wheels off
his daughter's bike.
We put yesterday out with the garbage
and wait for the delivery of tomorrow,
and we discover that
every day is a day of joy,
Spirit of Gladness.

Help us to play with you
each and every day,
God in Community, Holy and One,
even as we pray to you,
each and every day, saying …

The Lord's Prayer

Call to reconciliation:

In a world which teaches us always to be serious,
God gives us children who love to make silly faces.

In a world which searches for perfection,
God hands us the platypus.

Let us speak to God of our reluctance to be playful,
so we can be embraced by the One
who was willing to put aside divine dignity
to become one of us.

Prayer of forgiveness:

God of wonder,
you take mud, add a little water –
and make mountains,
while we worry about getting our clothes dirty playing outside.

You nourish your creation with refreshing rain,
and we grumble about having left our umbrellas at home.

You grin at the sight of squirrels chasing each other up and down trees,
and we can't remember the last time we lay down on the grass,
trying to guess what the clouds up in the sky look like.

Forgive us,
Imagination behind creation,
for forgetting to enjoy, to laugh, to play.
We take ourselves so seriously
that we lose sight of the wonder of your gifts.
We think you want us to be so proper all the time,
and so we have forgotten the joy, the laughter, the delight
which Jesus Christ, our Lord and Saviour,
brought into our lives.

Silence

Assurance of pardon:

The good news is this:
imagination and play go hand in hand with prayer,
with service, with worship, with life.
God takes delight when we take the time to enjoy
and play in
the good creation offered to us.
Amen

Great prayer of thanksgiving:

God be with you.
And also with you.

Open your hearts.
We open them to God.

Say 'thank you' to God.
We always want to thank God for everything.

Bunnies and butterflies,
dogs with muddy feet,
cats with whiskers that tickle,
frogs that jump a long way,
worms that inch along the sidewalk.
You made all this –
and so much more:

skies so blue we want to dive in,
fluffy clouds so soft and white,
mums who hold us when we are scared,
dads who throw us high into the air.
You made all this –
and so, so much more –
for us!

Thank you, God.
And hear as we sing with the angels
and all your children:

Sing two verses of 'Jesus loves me'.

God, you loved your child, Jesus,
and could have kept him close to you.
But you sent him to show us your love.
A little boy, he skinned his knees playing,
and liked his mum and dad to read him stories.

A teenager, he felt sort of clumsy,
and wondered what he would do
when he grew up.

When he got older,
he was a friend to people
who felt no one liked them;
he loved the people everybody else picked on;
he would gather up kids in his lap,
and tell them how much God loved them.

Then he died,
for his friends
and for those who didn't like him.

That's when God,
who loved his child so much,
brought him back to life,
just as God will give us new life
when we die.

And so, we sing about Jesus,
God's Child, our Friend, our Saviour:

Sing two verses of 'Away in the manger'.

Spirit of God,
you blow through the trees,
making the leaves dance;
you cool us off
on a hot summer day;
you whisper in our ears
about God's dreams for us.

So come now,
and make this bread we are about to eat
taste so good we want
to share it with everyone we meet.

Make the juice in the cup
so sweet and pure
that we want to go out
and tell others about
how much God loves them.
Thank you, Jesus, for loving us so much;
thank you, Holy Spirit, for helping us so much;
thank you, God, for being with us,
now and always.
Amen

Communion

Prayers of concern

Song

Blessing

If the weather is nice, go outside and share a picnic and play games.

Where you go, I will go

Readings and reflections for the UN International Day of Friendship (July 30)

Tom Gordon

May there always be work for your hands to do,
may your purse always hold a coin or two.
May the sun always shine on your windowpane,
may a rainbow be certain to follow each rain.
May the hand of a friend always be near you,
may God fill your heart with gladness to cheer you.

A Celtic blessing[1]

The hand of a friend

My grandmother lived till she was 95. After my grandfather died, she lived on her own well into her 90s in a tenement stair in the town of Paisley in Scotland. Though she was alone in her house, she always cooked for two. Stews, pot roasts, soups, pies were always made in double quantities. I once asked her why she did that, thinking it was because she couldn't break the fifty-year habit of preparing meals for her and her husband. 'Oh,' she replied, 'I always cook for old Jimmy as well.'

'Who's old Jimmy?' I enquired.

'Mr Davidson, old Jimmy Davidson. He lives across the hallway. He doesn't look after himself that well. He's been going downhill since his wife died. So I make meals for him, and then I know that he has at least one decent meal a day. I like old Jimmy. I think I'm the only friend he has.'

Jimmy Davidson – 'Old Jimmy' – was 69. My grandmother was 91. But she cared for him because the hand of friendship always mattered.

I remember my grandmother telling me a story about friendship when I was a little boy. She loved telling stories. I loved listening to them. And they always had a point to them. 'Once upon a time,' she would begin, 'long, long ago, in a deep jungle in a faraway land, there lived a great lion ...'

The lion and the mouse (after Aesop)

The lion was the king of the jungle, and all the other animals were afraid of him and always did as they were told. When the lion roared, all the creatures knew who was boss. The lion loved being king of the jungle. He was never frightened of anything, and always expected his subjects to be obedient to his roar.

So the lion ruled the jungle. Half the time he went out hunting. And half the time he slept. When he was hunting, all the creatures kept out of his way. And when he was at home, no animal dared to disturb him. No creature came near his den, especially when the lion was sleeping. For, if he was wakened, he would fly into a rage and roar so loudly the whole jungle shook. So all the animals in the jungle knew to leave the lion alone, because they were afraid of him.

One day a little mouse got curious. He wanted to see where the lion lived and what the king of the jungle's den was like. So he found the lion's den and waited for the lion to get back from his hunting. And he waited ... and waited ... and waited ... But the lion never appeared.

'Maybe he never went hunting today and he's still inside his den,' the mouse said to himself. And he waited ... and waited ... and waited some more.

'I'm fed up waiting,' said the mouse. 'I'm going to find out for myself.' And, with that, he sneaked into the lion's den. It was a dark place, a much bigger house than a little mouse had ever seen before. He felt very small and a little afraid when he saw the large footprints of the lion on the ground.

'Maybe I should turn back,' he muttered. Then ... he heard the pounding sound of the lion's footsteps.

'Oh no, he's coming back. What do I do now?' The little mouse shook with fear. He knew how angry the lion could get. The lion had only gone for a drink from the river close by and he was coming back for his sleep. So the mouse hid himself in a dark corner of the den while the lion sat near the entrance and rested his head on his huge paws. Soon he was fast asleep.

This was the mouse's chance to escape. So he crept as quietly as he could, till he was near the entrance. But the snoring lion was blocking his path.

'I'll have to climb over him,' he thought. 'But I'm very, very small, and the lion won't notice me when he's sleeping.'

So he tiptoed ever so carefully. Step by step, quietly, gently, he made his way over the big, sleeping lion. And he'd just about made it to safety when his little tail tickled the lion's nose, and the king of the jungle woke up with a start. Imagine his anger and the roar he gave when he saw there was a little mouse in his den.

Before the mouse could run away, the lion caught him by the tail, swung him into the air and, opening his big jaws, was ready to have the mouse for his dinner. But the mouse cried out, 'O king, please forgive me. I didn't mean to wake you. I was just fascinated to see the den of a king. I'm just a little mouse and I was curious. Please let me go this time. I shall never forget your greatness. And if I ever have the chance, I will help you in whatever way I can when things are bad for you.'

Now the lion was very amused at this. How can a little mouse help a lion? he thought. But he let him go anyway and roared with laughter. 'A mouse doing something to assist the king of the jungle? Ha! Ha! Ha!' And while the lion was laughing, the mouse ran for his life, thankful he could escape at last.

A few days later, as the lion was prowling through the jungle, it was suddenly caught in a hunter's snare. He struggled furiously to break free. But it was no use. He only got more tangled in the net of ropes. He roared with anger. But he was trapped for good. The whole jungle began to shake due to the terrible sound and every animal heard the lion's cries. The mouse heard it too.

The king of the jungle is in trouble, thought the mouse. Maybe I can help him, just as I promised. So he ran as fast as he could to the place where the sounds were coming from. And there was the lion, stuck in the hunter's net, and exhausted with his struggles to break free.

'Don't move, your majesty,' said the mouse, in the loudest and bravest voice he could find. 'I'll cut your ropes and get you free.' And without wasting a moment, he began nibbling through the ropes with his sharp little teeth. One by one the ropes were cut, and, after a while, the lion was freed from the trap.

'Thank you, Mr Mouse,' said the lion. 'I didn't believe that a little mouse could help the likes of me.' The great lion bowed down before the little mouse.

'Thank you for saving my life.' And the two creatures – the king of the jungle and a brave little mouse – became the best of friends from that day.

This wasn't just a story for my grandmother but an important lesson to pass on to her grandson. It was a message she lived by, a moral that defined her life. My grandmother was no mouse. And old Jimmy Davidson was no king. But when a need presented itself, the hand of friendship made such a difference. The importance of the hand of a friend transcends rank or position. It matters to the greatest among us and to the least. It is available to the weakest and most feeble among us, to be given and received, to the benefit of all.

My hands

There is work for my hands to do.
But what are these hands
when the rest of me is so small
and the tasks to fulfil are so great?

These hands are all I have.
These hands will have to be good enough.
These hands will offer love
to those who need it most.

There is love in my heart to show.
But when is this love going to be sufficient
when so much love is needed
by so many, many people?

This is the heart of love I have.
This loving heart will have to be good enough.
This heart will offer loving friendship
to those who need it most.

There is friendship in my life to show.
But how will this friendship be what's required
when so many friendless people
need something of the little that's mine?

This is the friendship I have.
This friendship will have to be good enough,
to be added to the hand of friendship of many others
and make an enormous difference.

The bosom of my family

A schoolclass of children, exploring with their teacher the importance of family, were asked to write a definition of 'a relative'. Among the expected emphases on blood-ties, ancestry, family trees and the like, one child offered this revealing statement:

'A relative is someone who comes to visit at your house who isn't a friend.'

When we experience the breakdown of family life, and love within our blood-ties is compromised, we are all the poorer. But when our best friends are within the bosom of a family, when deep friendship is enshrined in family relationships, how special it is.

Consider this story from the Book of Ruth:

> In the days when the judges ruled, there was a famine in the land. So a man from Bethlehem in Judah took his wife and two sons and left their own country and went to a foreign place, the country of Moab, in search of food and welfare. The father was Elimelek, Naomi was his wife and their two sons were Mahlon and Kilion. They were refugees from Bethlehem, and they were far from home in Moab. But at least it was a new beginning, and they lived there for a long while.
>
> In time, Elimelek died, leaving Naomi as a poor widow to bring up her two sons. She did well, and, settled in Moab, the young men grew up and married Moabite women, one named Orpah and the other Ruth. The family lived together for about ten years, and struggled on as best they could. But as if they hadn't lived with enough tragedy, both Mahlon and Kilion also died. Then word reached Naomi that things were better back in her own country. The people of her homeland had food again.
>
> 'My Lord has provided for His people,' she said.
>
> She got ready to go home, accompanied by her two daughters-in-law. So the three women prepared for their journey back to Judah. But Naomi was concerned for the two young women. They would be leaving their own country, and going to a land they didn't know, because their mother-in-law was choosing to go home.

So she said to her daughters-in-law, 'Go back, each of you, to your own family, to your mother's home. My Lord has shown kindness to me. May you know the same kindness in your own lives. My prayer is that you will find a new beginning, and perhaps marry again, and, above all, be happy.'

Then she kissed them goodbye. But as she did so, they wept aloud. 'No. Our loyalty is to you. We will go back with you to your people.'

But Naomi said, 'No. Go back home, my daughters. Why would you come with me? I'm not going to have any more sons. I cannot give you new husbands. I am too old to have another husband. Even if I thought there was still hope for me – even if I had a husband tonight and then gave birth to sons – would you wait until they grew up? Would you remain unmarried for them? No, my daughters. We have lived with sadness, and we will do so again. So, go home. It's your best chance of being happy.'

Still crying, Orpah kissed her mother-in-law goodbye. But Ruth hugged Naomi and wouldn't let her go.

'Look,' said Naomi, 'your sister-in-law is going back to her people and her religion. Go back with her.'

But Ruth was having none of it. 'Don't insist that I leave you or to turn back from you. Where you go I will go, and where you stay I will stay. Your people will be my people and your God my God. Where you die I will die, and there I will be buried. In God's name I will face whatever I have to face, even if death separates you and me.'

And Naomi realised there and then that Ruth was determined to go with her. So she stopped insisting. And she and Ruth travelled back to Judah.

(Ruth 1:1–18, the author's paraphrasing)

The importance of the hand of a friend isn't automatic in family relationships, or confined to our country of origin or defined within the context of our religion or cultural upbringing.

Which of us is not the better for having a friend who will go to the ends of the earth with us and for us?

The ends of the earth

The ends of the earth
are well within my reach.
They are mine to know.

The ends of the earth
are not foreign and strange.
They are like home to me.

The ends of the earth
are at the ends of my hands –
as close and as reachable as that.

The ends of the earth
are mine to claim
when my hands offer friendship.

The ends of the earth
need not be new and different
when my hands reach out in love.

The ends of the earth
are somewhere I must go
to accompany my friends.
The hand of friendship is universal.

All the great world religions have friendship enshrined within their codes and commandments, their teaching and their understanding of truth. But do religions not simply seek to define that which is fundamental to our humanity? Is the capacity to befriend, to see the need of another human being and to reach out in love, not part of our common humanity?

'Two doughnuts, please'

Snax@Mac's was the only café in the High Street. There were several outlets of well-known international chains too, of course. But many considered Snax@Mac's to be the only proper café in the centre of the town.

David McAndrew, the 'Mac' of the name, was proud of his establishment. He'd worked hard to transform it from the 'greasy spoon' kind of place it once was to the well-run, warm and welcoming place it was today.

Snax@Mac's was always busy, especially around lunchtime, and, as the genial and engaging host, Mac knew his regulars well. There were Andy, Chic and Frank, the lads from the tyre-and-exhaust garage a few doors down, with their banter, two filled rolls each and mugs of strong 'builder's brew'; there were the Mitchells and the Patersons, two elderly couples who met up at lunchtime without fail, and always ordered steak pie and chips all round; there were Karen and Louise, shop assistants from the newsagents across the road: two cheese burgers (one with onions and one without), two cans of cola and a half-hour of texting and giggles.

Mac had gleaned a fair bit of information about his regulars over the months. The friendly atmosphere in Snax@Mac's was important to him. But there was one of his regulars who puzzled him a lot.

Mac knew next to nothing about Greig, apart from the fact that he was in Snax@Mac's every day right on 11:30 – one cup of black coffee and two jam doughnuts ... one in a bag to be taken away, the other consumed with the coffee at the table by the window ... ten minutes, and no more than a hello, the placing of the order, a thank you, and a cursory goodbye.

Greig had been a regular for eighteen months or more, and Mac knew as much about Greig now as he did when he first came into the café – nothing whatsoever, apart, that is ... every day right on 11:30, one cup of black coffee, two jam doughnuts, one in a bag, etc, etc.

Mac had more than enough to think about keeping Snax@Mac's up to standard and making sure his regular and casual customers were happy with the only proper café in the High Street. But he couldn't help wondering occasionally, when Greig was exiting the café after his brief sojourn, what made this man tick, what he did for a living, why the regularity of his visits and their timing, and – just a passing thought – why the second jam doughnut?

All was revealed by chance one Wednesday morning. Mac was late because he'd had a dental appointment on the other side of town. Mac had made arrangements for the café to be covered by his wife, Penny, and her friend – able and willing stand-ins. Mac had parked his car and was walking down to the café not long after 11:30. Well, it must have been exactly 11:40, for there was Greig exiting Snax@Mac's right on time, clutching the familiar white paper bag which Mac knew held the second of two jam doughnuts. And he was intrigued to see Greig duck up the alleyway next to the garage and return a minute or so later – without the bag with the doughnut. Interesting, *very* interesting thought Mac.

When Greig came into Snax@Mac's the next day right on 11:30 – one cup of black coffee, two doughnuts, one in a bag, etc, etc – Mac wondered if he should ask. He decided not to. But he didn't stop being intrigued.

So, on the Friday, he asked Penny and her friend to look after the café for an hour between 11 and 12, and stood across the road – and watched. Bang on 11:30 he saw Greig slip into the café, right on time. At 11:40, he saw him come out clutching the familiar white paper bag. And he watched him duck up the alleyway next to the garage and return a minute or so later – without the bag with the second doughnut.

As Greig walked off up the High Street, Mac slipped up the alleyway, and halfway up he found the reason for Greig's detour – for there, sitting on the ground, beside the bins at the back door of the tyre-and-exhaust centre, was an old down-and-out carefully savouring the last remnants of a jam doughnut.[2]

Friendship is shown in small ways and in big ones. It is personal and it is international. It is private and it is public. But in all of its varieties, it is simply about seeing our yearnings in the needs of others, stepping out of selfishness and giving ourselves away.

No matter what

Remind me,
when I get cynical and lose my faith in goodness,
that there are still friends who care,
no matter what.

Remind me,
when I get bitter and turn in on myself,
that there are still friends who turn outwards to others,
no matter what.

Remind me,
when I get selfish and no one matters but me,
that there are still friends who put others first,
no matter what.

Remind me,
when I get too busy and fail to look around me,
that there are still friends who have time to love,
no matter what.

Remind me,
when I get weary with well-doing and give up trying,
that there are still friends who never stop,
no matter what.

Sources:

1. Source unknown

2. Adapted from 'Two doughnuts, please', in *A Blessing to Follow: Contemporary Parables for Living*, by Tom Gordon, Wild Goose Publications, 2009

An ordinary day

Joy Mead

'To live at all is miracle enough'

– Title of a poem by Mervyn Peake

Awaking:

As we greet with wonder and uncertainty
the coming and the happenings of this new day

How can we keep from singing?

As we see holiness in ordinary places
where people in all their depth and mystery
work and play, laugh and cry;
where life is cherished, sustained
and handed on

How can we keep from singing?

As we oppose all that denies life
in its fullness and variety,
in our lives, our communities, our world

How can we keep from singing?

As we weep over injustice
rejoice in goodness
love outrageously

How can we keep from singing?

As we affirm our hope for tomorrow
and our faith in the indefinable

How can we keep from singing?

Silence, or singing: 'Oh the life of the world', Kathy Galloway, *Iona Abbey Music Book*, Wild Goose Publications

Seeking:

God, the promise of life in little bodies and tiny seeds,
We seek eyes that wonder at the mystery of the earth.

God, the promise of life in the fragile wings of a butterfly,
We seek to know our part in the intricate pattern of being.

God, the promise of life in a child's trusting hands,
We seek to make the way of wholeness and peace.

God, the promise of life in friendship and companionship,
We seek to understand the miracle of every shared meal.

Silence

Lamenting:

The joy of the morning
and the sorrow of the day
are interwoven.

Lament ...

Sing a song of sadness:

for the miseries of the world
that venom every hour;

for people dying,
unheeded, untended,
from weather, hunger
and the ways of men;

for children crying
where nobody hears;

for people turned away
from places they dream
of calling home;

for people sick and uncared for,
dirty and unkempt;

for people oppressed
and longing for justice.

Sing a song of sadness:

for farmers who are lured to buy
hybrid cotton seeds, white gold,
to make them millionaires,
then kill themselves with pesticides
they can't afford;

for the knowledge of the people
being converted into the property
of global corporations;

for the perverted view
that sees bees as thieves
stealing pollen.

Sing a song of sadness:

for the neglect and abuse
of the earth and pollution
of the sweet waters;

for air unfit for breathing,
soil unfit for growing,
and the memory
of sweet apple scent.

Sing a song of sadness

walking across a field
in the last light
of a summer evening.

Silence, or singing: 'Over my head', from *Love and Anger*, John L. Bell and Graham Maule, Wild Goose Publications

Prayer:

Spirit of shadows and echoes, darkness and light
help us to be still in our dark moments,
our waiting times, our uncertainties
so that we may hear in the silence
the music of humanity.

Reflecting on the day's possibilities:

The Buddha was once asked, 'What makes a person holy?' He replied, 'Every hour is divided into a certain number of seconds and every second into a certain number of fractions. Anyone who is able to be totally present in each fraction of a second is holy.' There is nothing common about common life – it takes an awakened sense to see what is mysterious in each ordinary moment, to ponder in our hearts, to *really* see, people and things – not our preconceptions of them.

So on the threshold of a new day, look slowly and listen to the heartbeat of life, be guided by love with justice and what makes our whole being sing; step out into the uncertainty celebrating, trusting and open to each precious moment.

Prayer:

God of words and wonderings
we are thankful for:
insights that show us
   straight lines are overrated,
   logic and reason don't solve everything,
   the table is round,
   and there's music in the air;
quiet moments, noisy moments, inspiring moments,

voices that echo in our minds,
and become friends;
all-sorted conversations;
seeds that don't stay
where they are put;

friends who encourage walking on air,
which is not an element for walking on;
earth-supported, water-washed, air-blessed, fire-inspired
bread and poetry;
space to shape something
both beautiful and useful;
connections and process;
being and becoming;
today and tomorrow, which are different,
and always will be.

Blessing and going out:

Love, tangible and expressive,
Transform us.

Joy, holy and earthy,
Uplift us.

Peace, of heart, home and community,
Be within us, always.

May we never lose sight
of the possibility of transformation
and be continually surprised
by people who believe in one another.

Moving house

A basic liturgy for saying goodbye

Kes Grant

Adapt as necessary.

Loving God,
we thank you that you shelter us under your wings.
Today we give thanks for the shelter that this house has provided *(name)*
for ____ years.

We give thanks for the bricks that have weathered many storms,
both inside and out.
Help *(name)* rest secure in the faith
that you will continue to surround and protect her,
wherever she finds herself.

As we move around the house together
we feel the memories of the years.
Today is a day to give thanks for those memories *(name)* carries with her,
as well as take the time to lay to rest those
she no longer needs to carry ...

In this living room,
we give thanks for shared laughter and love,
for relaxing evenings and times spent with family and friends.
We lay aside difficult conversations and phone calls
that have hurt and wounded *(name)*
and evenings spent doubting ...

God of the universe,
inspire us and move us on.

In this kitchen,
we give thanks for all that has sustained and nourished *(name)*
over the years.
We also thank you for the culinary creations shared with friends and family,
as well as the hurried bites whilst dashing
to important events and meetings.
We lay aside those days when *(name)* didn't take the time
she needed for herself ...

God of the universe,
inspire us and move us on.

In this bedroom,
we thank you for the rest that has sustained *(name)* in body, mind and soul.
We are glad for the time to dream dreams and make them a reality.
As we leave this room
we also leave behind all nightmares and sleepless nights
and ask you to banish *(name's)* fears …

God of the universe,
inspire us and move us on.

In this bathroom,
we give thanks for the pampering that *(name)* has given herself and others.
For the care and attention she has shown herself
and the compassion shared with others.
We thank you for bubbles and candles and treats.
We leave behind insecurities about ourselves
that we see staring back at us in the mirror,
and ask you to fill *(name)* with confidence
and your transforming light and love …

God of the universe,
inspire us and move us on.

At this front door,
we thank you for all who have supported and upheld *(name)* over the years.
For the people who have come and gone
and left footprints in *(name's)* heart.
As she steps over this threshold for the last time
help her to breathe in the love of all who believe in her
and to breathe out any fear and anxiety …

May she step out in faith and hope
and be open to all that is to come.

God of the universe,
inspire us and move us on.
Amen

The heart of things

An all-age exploration of the Prodigal Son

Nancy Cocks

Introduction:

In the symbolic action of this service folk are invited to create paper hearts that stretch. Two patterns (large heart, small hearts) are available to download from the links below; and there is a video link which shows and explains how to make 'hearts that stretch'. Have fun. (If you don't want to make hearts there is an alternate to this action.)

Large heart: http://www.ionabooks.com/content/wp-content/uploads/2018/10/Large-heart.pdf

Small hearts: http://www.ionabooks.com/content/wp-content/uploads/2018/10/Small-hearts.pdf

Instructions for making a heart that stretches (the action): www.ionabooks.com/content/the-heart-of-things-an-all-age-exploration-of-the-prodigal-son-by-nancy-cocks/

The leader needs the large heart and a pair of scissors.

Note to Leader: practise making your heart in advance so you know what you're doing when you make your heart in the service! Children are quite impressed by how far a paper heart can stretch but you don't want the heart to tear apart. So, please, practise. Everyone else gets a small heart. Have a supply of safety scissors available.

Welcome

Song: 'He's got the whole world in his hands', or another well-known song about God's all-embracing love

We say good morning to God:

God, we are glad to think you have the whole world in your hands. Your love stretches far enough to reach every person and every creature, great or small. Each one is precious to you. Thank you that your love is so strong that it will never let us go. You have promised us this in Jesus and so we are glad to greet you today in his name. Amen

A conversation: what is love?:

Hand out the small paper hearts to the children (one each). The conversation leader could also bring along some old greeting cards with hearts on them: Valentine, engagement or wedding, anniversary, birthday, thank you cards …

- When do we give each other hearts? … (Show the cards at this point if the children don't have a lot of answers of their own.)
- What does giving or receiving a heart tells us? …
  Use the children's examples to focus on the different times we say to each other: 'I love you' or 'You are very special.'
- So what is love?…
  A special feeling for somebody special.
  An action that tells us we're special.
- What kinds of actions show somebody loves us? …
  A hug, a kiss, giving a gift, doing a favour …
  Cards show different kinds of love between people.
  Love between people who get married; love between friends; love between parents and children …

- Who loves you, would you say? …
  Always good to have someone who loves us!

- And how do you treat someone who loves you? …

Jesus told a story about love in a family and how that love sometimes gets tested.

Listen to the first part of the story.

The story of the younger son:

Paraphrased from the NRSV

Jesus told this story:

There was a man who had two sons. The younger son said to his father, 'Dad, I have a plan and I need money. So give me my share of what you'll leave me when you're gone.' The father wasn't happy but he gave his younger son what he asked for.

A few days later the younger son took everything he owned and left home. He went far away. And in a far-off country, he spent everything his father gave him. Then times got tough and he had nothing left. So he found a job with a pig farmer, work no one else would do. He had to feed those pigs every day but no one gave him anything to eat.

So at last the younger son thought to himself, *My father's hired hands all have more than enough to eat, but here I am dying of hunger! I think I'll go home and talk to my father. 'Dad,' I'll say, 'I have done you wrong. I'm not worthy to be called your son any more: treat me like one of your hired hands. Just give me a job, please.'*

And so he set off for home.

But while he was still far away from his father's house, his father saw him. This dad felt so sorry for his son. And he was so glad to see him again! So this dad, he ran, threw his arms around his son and kissed him. The son began the speech he'd been practising: 'Dad, I have done you wrong. I'm not worthy to be called your son –'

But before the son could finish, the father said to his servants, 'Go, bring out the nicest jacket for him. Put a ring on his finger and new sandals on his feet. And get the roast to barbecue. Tonight we celebrate! For this son of mine, who I thought was gone for good, is part of the family again: he was lost and now he is found!'

And they began to party.

Talking about the story:

Now that young man didn't exactly treat his dad with love, did he?

He did all kinds of things parents warn children not to do!

So when he wanted to go home, he wondered if his dad would take him back.

Sometimes, when we know we've done something that makes our parents unhappy, we wonder if they still love us.

Sometimes, when we have done something wrong and things have fallen apart, we can be afraid nothing will ever go right again.

So Jesus told us this story to remind us that God loves us *so* much; God will always give us a second chance.

Like that father, God is always glad to welcome us back home!

So if something ever goes really wrong for you, remember that never means it's the end of the story.

With God's love we can always make a new beginning.

So now let's say sorry to God for anything we've done that we might be worried about:

We say sorry to God (said all together):

Dear God, some days we have to admit that being part of a family is hard work. Parents watch children do something they think is unwise and they worry, they scold, they warn. Other days, children see parents do something they think is unwise and they grumble, they worry, they don't know what to do. God, we are sorry for those times we've made it hard for our own family to get along. Show us the way to forgive each other, just as you forgive us.

We hear God's promise of love:

Dear friends, while it is true we have all made a mess of our lives in some way, it is also true that God forgives us when we own up to what we've done. With Jesus' love we can become new people. So know that we make God glad when we remember to say we're sorry. Feel God's forgiveness today as we sing – for that is the heart of things for all Jesus' friends!

Song: Sing a cheerful Alleluia that everyone knows, or can learn easily.

The story of the older son:

Leader: But now the story gets even more interesting! That young brother had an older brother and he had something to say. Listen:

Now the older brother was in the field when his younger brother returned. When he came back to the house, he heard music and dancing. He called one of the servants and asked what was going on.

'Sir, your brother has come home. Your father laid on this big party because he is home, safe and sound.'

Well, the older brother was really angry. 'Harrumph! I'm not going to this party!'

So his father came out and begged him to come in.

But the big brother argued, 'Listen, Dad! For years I've done all the work for you. I've never let you down. Yet you have never given me a party with my friends. But when this son of yours comes home, the one who has wasted all the money you gave him, you roll out the red carpet for him!'

His father shook his head. 'Son, you are always with me. Everything I own now is yours. But we had to celebrate today. Your brother was dead to us. But now he has come back to life. He was lost and now he's found.'

Thinking about the story:

That's where the story ends. We have to decide how it works out.

What would that older brother do, do you think?

Would he come to the party for his younger brother?

Or would he stay mad, afraid his dad loved his brother more than him?

Think about it as we listen to our drama.

Drama: Mum always loved you best

For four parts: Mother Frog, Fergie the Frog, Grandma Frog and a narrator.

Mother: Fergie? Are you ready? It's time to go!

Narrator: Fergie the Frog just sat there, frowning.

Mother: Fergie, it's time to watch Freddie in the fly-catching finals. Hop to it!

Fergie: I'm not going!

Mother: Why not? Your brother could win a trophy today. It will be very exciting.

Fergie: I'm tired of Freddie.

Mother: Then you will have to go to Grandma's ...

Fergie: All right. That's better than watching stupid old Freddie and his stupid old tongue.

Mother: Ferguson! Watch *your* tongue.

Narrator: So off they hopped: Fergie to his grandmother's, and the rest of the family to Swamp Stadium.

When Fergie got to his grandmother's, she was very glad to see him. She kissed him on his nose and didn't seem to notice when Fergie made a face.

Grandma: I baked your favourite cookies, Fergie. Oatmeal with chopped beetle chips.

Fergie: *(frowning)* Those are Freddie's favourite cookies. My favourites are mosquito jam roll-ups.

Grandma: I'm sorry, Fergie. I'll make those next time you come.

Narrator: Fergie sighed as he captured a cookie with the flick of his tongue.

Fergie: *(still frowning)* Freddie is everybody's favourite frog.

Narrator: Grandma Frog blinked at Fergie.

Grandma: Now what makes you say that?

Fergie: Mum and dad go to Freddie's competitions all the time. It's Freddie this and Freddie that. They put his trophies on the round rock table. But they make *me* do my homework. Mum and dad love Freddie best because he has the longest tongue in the family. *You* love Freddie best because you made his favourite cookies.

Narrator: Fergie frowned at his toes.

Grandma: Fergie, you can't tell who loves you by cookies or trophies or tongues. I will still love Freddie whether he wins or loses today. And your mum and dad love you without trophies. They love you for yourself, not the length of your tongue.

Fergie: … Do you think so? Even if I can't catch flies very well?

Grandma: Yes! Even if you have the shortest tongue a frog ever flicked.

Narrator: Fergie thought for a moment. Then he smiled and zapped another cookie with his tongue.

Fergie: Grandma, I'm going to do you a favour today. I'm going to eat every single one of these beetle-chip cookies – all by myself.

Narrator: His grandmother looked surprised.

Fergie: Then when Freddie gets here, you will know that he loves you for yourself, and not just for your cookies!

Talking about the stories:

- It's a hard thing in families if we ever think our parents or our grandparents love someone else in the family more than they love us. It hurts when we think someone else is the favourite.
- Or we can get worried if we think somebody else is the favourite in our class, on our team, in the neighbourhood. We worry we don't matter very much.
- So if you ever feel that way, please remember God has more than enough love to go around for everybody.
- God doesn't love anybody more than anyone else. There's always enough of God's love to go around!
- So let's sing a song to remind us about God's love for us.

Song: 'Jesus loves me', or another song about God's love which the children know

Offering: The leader might make the point that the offering is one way we give our love back to God.

Symbolic action:

Leader: Sometimes our hearts need stretching!

God's people trust that there is always enough love to go around.

That's why everybody has a heart to take home today.

There is enough love for everyone here.

But if we're going to share God's love, we might have to stretch our own hearts to fit other people into our love.

How many people do you think could fit inside this heart *(holding up the big heart)*?

Would you fit inside ... two? More?

The small hearts seem too small even for one person!

The leader then demonstrates how to make a big heart that stretches ... Then tries to fit the big heart around a few of the children.

Leader: Now you see that hearts filled with Jesus' love can stretch to make more room for more and more people.

Sometimes we have to stretch our hearts to make room for others, like the older brother in Jesus' story. He needed to stretch his heart and welcome his little brother back.

Sometimes our hearts need stretching, too, so we remember to love someone we've been angry with or jealous of, or someone who seems different than our other friends.

When your heart needs stretching, remember Jesus' story about the father who had more than enough love for his whole family.

God's heart is big enough to fit us all!

Action: making hearts that stretch

You might want to have folk in groups, with leaders demonstrating how to make the hearts. Take your time and be sure to include everyone.

Note: As an alternative to the action, you could set aside a bit of space here for folk to sit and think about the people they love, about God's unconditional love, and about opening their hearts wider for folk they find it hard to love or like, or who are excluded in the world. Play some gentle music during this.

Prayers from our hearts:

Where the dots appear near the end of each prayer, pause briefly for silent prayer, before giving the cue for the song.

Prayer song: 'Come, bring your burdens to God', from *We Walk His Way*, John L. Bell, Wild Goose Publications (teach this at the beginning of the service)

O God, we pray this day for all whose hearts are heavy and sad, for people who don't feel like singing … Lord, carry all our hurts as we sing:

Song

O God, we pray for all whose hearts are filled with worry or fear. And for everyone who lives somewhere in danger … Lord, carry all our fears as we sing:

Song

O God, we pray for those who are sick and for those who look after them … Lord, carry all our pain as we sing:

Song

O God, we pray for people who are hungry and people who need to find work … Lord, carry all our need as we sing:

Song

O God, we pray for our families, for things that have gone wrong and things we'd like to set right ... Help us tell each other of the love in our hearts. Lord, carry all our love as we sing:

Song

Closing song: 'Draw the circle wide', or any song about God's amazing love – something upbeat to send folk on their way rejoicing

The colour of love

Resources for World AIDS Day (December 1st)

Tom Gordon

People like us

> *'The physician should treat not only the disease but the patient who is suffering from it.'*
>
> *Moshe ben Maimon ('Maimonides') 1135-1204*

World AIDS Day was held for the first time in 1988. So for almost 30 years, this global health day has encouraged all of us to show support for people living with HIV and to remember those who have died. AIDS is a modern-day scourge, affecting thousands of people in the UK and tens of millions throughout the world. There have been advances in treatment, of course, and there is more tolerance and a greater understanding of the disease and the risks of contracting HIV. But 30 years on from the first World Aids Day, humanity still needs to stop and reflect on the effect of this major pandemic on the welfare of our world.

But perhaps the most important aspect of World AIDS Day is the message enshrined in the quotation from Maimonides which begins this reflection. We should not only treat the disease, but also continue to focus on the living person behind that disease and treat them too. HIV and AIDS still need to be talked about. Behind the AIDS and HIV there is a person, and that person still matters.

So on World AIDS Day, let's think about the person as well as the illness. Let's deal with our prejudices as well as the disease. Let's dispel the stigma as well as finding new treatments. World AIDS Day is about people, and, in our common humanity, we remember that they are people like us.

I see, I know

I see a black skin, different from mine,
and I think I know the difference.

But do I?

Is this person really different from me?
Or does focusing on skin colour
get in the way of our common humanity?

I see disability, a body functioning differently from mine,
and I think I know the difference.

But do I?

Is this person really different from me?
Or does my failure to accept varied abilities
get in the way of our acceptance of one another?

I see behaviour, different from mine,
and I think I know the difference.

But do I?

Is this person really different from me?
Or does my lack of understanding of their circumstances
get in the way of tolerance?

I see someone differently labelled, living with a disease,
and I think I know the difference.

But do I?

Is this person really different from me?
Or do I need to see them as they are,
me, in them – or am I getting in the way?

The red ribbon

The use of a coloured ribbon to indicate that the wearer is a supporter of a particular charity or campaign has become commonplace in recent years. It's almost universal now, and the range of colours and the meanings applied to them is quite remarkable.

Perhaps the most ubiquitous ribbon – and certainly one of the earliest – is the red ribbon worn as a symbol of awareness of, and support for, those living with AIDS and HIV. The use of the red ribbon began in the early 1990s, a decade or so after the emergence of HIV as a major worldwide problem. Red was chosen because it's bold and visible, and symbolises love and passion.

Some years ago my wife and I were walking along one of Edinburgh's busy shopping streets, when we were accosted by a photographer. I was about to dismiss him impatiently when I heard him say that he wanted to take my photograph because I was wearing an AIDS ribbon. He'd been commissioned to take photos of random people wearing red ribbons, he explained, to show that the awareness of HIV had gone right down to the grassroots of our society. So my photograph was duly taken, and, in time, I appeared on a publicity poster along with a couple of dozen other people all wearing their red ribbons. And with the cleverness of such things – too technical for me to understand – the people in the poster and the city street behind us had been reduced to various shades of grey, and the only colour that was left was the red of the ribbons.

The ribbons mattered more than the people who were wearing them and the street in which they went about their business. The red ribbons stood out from everything else. On World AIDS Day, they continue to do so.

Red

This reflection will work best with two voices. During the silences there may be some action, such as the lighting of candles on an altar or central table, or the pinning of red ribbons on a board or central display.

Red ... the colour of extremes –
from danger to love,
from violence to adventure,

from seduction to anger,
from a loving heart to a wounded body.

And a red ribbon stands out on World AIDS Day – as we identify with those who live with the extremes of HIV.

(Silence)

Red ... the colour of life –
fire, and vigour, and purpose,
primal forces and basic energy,
the morning sky and the setting sun,
the beating heart and flowing blood.

And a red ribbon stands out on World AIDS Day – as we remember those who cling preciously to the preciousness of life.

(Silence)

Red ... the colour of magic and religion –
Greek heroism and Christian crucifixion,
scarves for good fortune throughout Asia,
saris for marriages in Nepal,
kimonos for good luck in Japan.

And a red ribbon stands out on World AIDS Day – as we reflect on those who look for good fortune through their chosen life-stance.

(Silence)

Red ... the colour of direction –
Stop signs and danger warnings,
sex-for-sale and a fall in stock market prices,
socialism and slipping into debt,
the hazard-indicator and the brake lights of a car.

And a red ribbon stands out on World AIDS Day – as we show support for those who seek to direct people to a better understanding.

(Silence)

Red ... the colour of standing out –
British phone boxes and London buses,
Santa Claus and the circus clown,
the Palace Guard and the fiery cross,
the red, red robin that's still bob bob bobbin' along.

And a red ribbon stands out on World AIDS Day – as we rally alongside those who stand firm for justice, and equity, and an end to prejudice.

(Silence)

Red ... the colour of power –
the business tie and the celebrity-trod carpet,
the badge of courage and the airborne display team,
paratroopers and politics,
national flags and military police.

And a red ribbon stands out on World AIDS Day – as we pray for those who seek the power of peace to change the world for the better.

(Silence)

Red ... the colour of description –
the herring and the town to be painted,
those tired eyes from an overnight flight,
the flag in a Communist anthem,
the ruby, the Cross and Crescent, the reindeer's nose.

And a red ribbon stands out on World AIDS Day – as we weep with those who would offer us a vivid description of their pain and suffering.

(Silence)

Red ... the colour of love –
the heart on a Valentine's Card,
the bunch of birthday roses,
the romantic lighting in an intimate place,
the first colour of a rainbow.

And a red ribbon stands out on World AIDS Day – as we offer love for those who have none; our love ... because, on World AIDS Day, love has to stand out above all else.

Soup and sundaes

For many years the Church of Scotland has offered the people of Scotland, through the work of its congregations, an educational HIV programme: www.churchofscotland.org.uk/serve/world_mission/hiv_programme.

Perhaps one of the most imaginative aspects of the Church's HIV programme is the development of 'Souper Sunday'. This provides an opportunity for people to share reflections on AIDS and HIV in an act of worship, before moving to a church hall or other local venue for a basic meal of soup and bread. The thinking behind this is simple: prayers and worship around the AIDS theme are fine, but it is better if people can talk, and learn, and share together, and, in addition, raise much needed funds for the Church's ongoing work.

But human nature being what it is, not everyone likes soup! 'Too one-dimensional,' some say. So rather than the non-soup-lovers opting out or feeling alienated, some congregations went on to develop 'Sundae Sunday'. It speaks for itself. Everyone likes ice cream, don't they?

So 'Sundae Sunday' serves the same purpose. Worship over, people can continue to learn together – and money can be raised – when they share their sundaes. Everyone benefits – including those with a sweet tooth – but, more especially, those who are living with HIV.

A grace for Souper Sunday

We're glad we have soup; we'll sip and we'll slurp,
and empty our plates pretty soon.
But what of the many with no plate or cup,
and nothing to put on their spoon?

So, God bless our soup; thank God for our meal;
for those who have made it we pray.
And God bless the people whose life's an ordeal –
all those who'll go hungry today.
Amen

A grace for Sundae Sunday

We're glad we have ice cream to spoon from a plate
or lick from a cone as a treat.
But what of the many who still have to wait
for some crumbs that might fall at their feet?

So, God bless our sundaes; our banquet is spread;
with aaahhhs and some mmmms we will pray!
And God bless the folk who don't even have bread,
who'll go to bed hungry today.
Amen

Naaman and leprosy

In the Bible, in the second book of Kings, we find this remarkable story. There are three principal characters: Naaman, a commander in the army of the king of Aram; one of the servant girls from the Kingdom of Israel, who attended to Naaman's wife; and Elisha, a man of God, a prophet of Israel.

The Bible story is about leprosy. But it has always struck me that it could equally be about HIV, or any other pandemic disease. As such, it is not only a story about cure, for it raises the issues of prejudice and judgement, ignorance and fear, healing and wholeness. Above all it reminds me that struggling with the effects, personal or societal, of a disease such as HIV is not confined to one stratum, class or economic group, but is something which has to be understood as affecting us all.

2 Kings 5:1–19 (New International Version):

Naaman was commander of the army of the king of Aram. He was a great man in the sight of his master and highly regarded, because through him the Lord had given victory to Aram. He was a valiant soldier, but he had leprosy.

Now bands of raiders from Aram had gone out and had taken captive a young girl from Israel, and she served Naaman's wife. She said to her mistress, 'If only my master would see the prophet who is in Samaria! He would cure him of his leprosy.' Naaman went to his master and told him what the girl from Israel had said. 'By all means, go,' the king of Aram replied. 'I will send a letter to the king of Israel.'

So Naaman left, taking with him ten talents of silver, six thousand shekels of gold and ten sets of clothing. The letter that he took to the king of Israel read: 'With this letter I am sending my servant Naaman to you so that you may cure him of his leprosy.'

As soon as the king of Israel read the letter, he tore his robes and said, 'Am I God? Can I kill and bring back to life? Why does this fellow send someone to me to be cured of his leprosy? See how he is trying to pick a quarrel with me!' When Elisha the man of God heard that the king of Israel had torn his robes, he sent him this message: 'Why have you torn your robes? Make the man come to me and he will know that there is a prophet in Israel.'

So Naaman went with his horses and chariots and stopped at the door of Elisha's house. Elisha sent a messenger to say to him, 'Go, wash yourself seven times in the Jordan, and your flesh will be restored and you will be cleansed.' But Naaman went away angry and said, 'I thought that he would surely come out to me and stand and call on the name of the Lord his God, wave his hand over the spot and cure me of my leprosy. Are not Abana and Pharpar, the rivers of Damascus, better than all the waters of Israel? Couldn't I wash in them and be cleansed?' So he turned and went off in a rage.

Naaman's servants went to him and said, 'My father, if the prophet had told you to do some great thing, would you not have done it? How much more, then, when he tells you, "Wash and be cleansed"!' So he went down and dipped himself in the Jordan seven times, as the man of God had told him, and his flesh was restored and became clean like that of a young boy.

Then Naaman and all his attendants went back to the man of God. He stood before him and said, 'Now I know that there is no God in all the world except in Israel. So please accept a gift from your servant.' The prophet answered, 'As surely as the Lord lives, whom I serve, I will not accept a thing.' And even though Naaman urged him, he refused. 'If you will not,' said Naaman, 'please let me, your servant, be given as much earth as a pair of mules can carry, for your servant will never again make burnt offerings and sacrifices to any other god but the Lord. But may the Lord forgive your servant for this one thing: when my master enters the temple of Rimmon to bow down and he is leaning on my arm and I have to bow there also – when I bow down in the temple of Rimmon, may the Lord forgive your servant for this.'

'Go in peace,' Elisha said.[1]

A prayer of awareness

This prayer could be used immediately after the above story is read, with two alternating voices.

Today, I am Naaman,
struck down,
unprotected by wealth and position,
open to the brokenness of humanity,
like everyone else.

Creating God,
make me more aware of who I am,
and what I feel,
and where I am in humanity's patterns.

Today, I am a servant girl,
doing my best,
filling my place,
yet knowing more than I'm expected to,
of goodness and healing.

Accepting God,
make me more aware of who I am,
and what I know,
and what I have to offer beyond myself.

Today, I am a foreign king,
apprehensive,
unsure of motives and obligations,
yet seeing beyond role
and human boundaries.

Embracing God,
make me more aware of who I am,
and where I stand,
and the barriers I can break down.

Today, I am Elisha the prophet,
standing firm,
with wisdom to offer
beyond my understanding
or the knowledge of anyone else.

Enlivening God,
make me more aware of who I am,
and where my faith lies,
and the wisdom I can bring that's beyond my comprehension.

Today, I am Naaman,
raised up,
healed in humility,
given a new start and a new hope
I never knew possible.

Loving God,
make me more aware of who I am,
and what I have,
and what is possible for me.

Out of sight, out of mind

In my home city of Edinburgh, HIV is not talked about nearly as much as it was several years ago. Newly developed drug therapies, better care and attention during times of acute illness and a better social understanding has meant that HIV and AIDS are no longer words that are regularly seen in the press or heard in news or current affairs programmes. They are no longer part of our regular conversations.

It may be a case, however, of 'out of sight, out of mind', because people still suffer, families are still broken and victims still die. Above all, prejudices are still expressed. And this is particularly true when HIV raises its head outwith the circles with which it is normally associated – in the drug culture or through unprotected sex. When someone contracts HIV through contaminated blood products, for example, and HIV and AIDS are no longer confined to the 'darker' sections of society, people who never expected to have to deal with such issues find the same prejudices others have known for decades.

Some years ago when I was working as a parish minister I struggled with my own reluctance to face up to the issue and to encourage my congregation to examine their own prejudices. Simply put, I was fearful of criticism that focusing on this aspect of the 'social gospel' might lead to me being criticised by the more traditional and less tolerant sections of my town-centre congregation.

I wrote a story about this in one of my books, a story which I put into the third person in order to protect myself. It was a true story, but I wasn't brave enough to be clear that it was about me. Now that I have worked through the issues and my own fearfulness, I offer the story again. But now I share it in the first person. I've learned to own the issue, with the hope that the core of the story – dealing with our prejudices – remains as vital as it has always been.

Crying with Mrs Henderson

I was having a bad day, and it being a Sunday, the day when I was expected to be on top of my game, made it all the worse. Two of my kids had been up half the night with their coughing. I was convinced I was coming down with flu myself. It was bucketing with rain when I left the house and walked to the church. And I knew that I was far from adequately prepared for the Sunday service.

In truth, I was having a bad week. As minister in my town-centre parish I'd had one of those weeks which every minister dreads. There had been three funerals to prepare and conduct, and the death of one of my best church members made at least one of the losses all too personal. There had been a difficult church meeting on the Monday when I had to cope with bickering and tensions as decisions had to be made about the redevelopment of the church hall and meeting rooms. It had become a veritable battleground between the traditionalists and the modernists, with me in the middle as usual. And I'd had a letter of criticism about the choice of my hymns the previous Sunday – a 'what-happened-to-all-the-good-old-hymns' kind of letter.

All of which meant that, in terms of preparation for the Sunday morning service, I just wasn't on top of my game. I was relieved, however, that I had some ready-made material to work with.

It was World AIDS Day, and, mercifully, the Church of Scotland had prepared some useful worship material in a new resource pack. There were specially written prayers, suggestions for Bible readings, words for a new hymn, notes for other items of praise, and – best of all – the bones of an appropriate sermon. I'd intended to adapt the sermon and put things in my own words. But, as a stressed-out minister at the end of a bad week, I'd been reduced to trusting the material in the resource pack and offering it largely as it was.

I knew I was falling short of my own high standards and expectations. So my inadequate preparation made me feel worse and worse during the worship service itself. In addition, I just *knew* that some of the material in the resource pack sermon wasn't going to go down well with the traditionalists in the congregation.

When it came to the sermon – 'fifteen minutes of your ministry being on the line', an old professor had once reminded his class of divinity students – and guided by the excellent resource material, I just 'went for it'. I talked forcibly of the scourge of HIV and AIDS in Africa. I explained how the retroviral drugs had little chance of working unless people were adequately fed. I suggested that our complacency had to be challenged – and I just *knew* there would be those who would complain about 'all this social justice stuff' that they'd heard more than enough of already.

I encouraged people not to be judgmental of those who contracted HIV through the sharing of dirty needles in an all-too-familiar drug culture. I shared insights into the care needed for HIV babies born to parents with AIDS and how these innocent little ones had to be given every chance – but I just *knew* there would be mutterings about 'pandering to people who'd caused their own problems'.

I called for the Church to be inclusive and for people to think of the damage done to those in the gay community who felt rejected by the Church's stance on same-sex relationships. I pleaded for compassionate church folk not to believe that AIDS was God's punishment for an 'abnormal' sexual orientation – and I just *knew* that someone, even now, would be forming a letter of complaint about the Church abandoning the True Gospel.

By the time the worship was over, I felt terrible. And as I smiled at people and shook hands with them as they left the church, I could just *feel* members of the congregation ready to add to my misery. It had been a bad service on a bad day, at the end of a bad week.

When I came back inside after people had gone, I noticed Mrs Henderson still in her place in the back row. Mrs Henderson was a quiet-spoken lady who came to church every Sunday. I didn't know her too well. But as I came closer to her, I saw that she had her head in her hands and that her eyes were closed. I decided that it was better not to disturb her, and chose to slip quietly past her down the side aisle. It didn't work. As I was passing, Mrs Henderson lifted her head.

'Mr Gordon,' she said, 'have you got a minute?' I stopped, my heart sinking with the expectation that even a mousy person like Mrs Henderson was going to give me a hard time for my sermon content or my lack of preparation.

'Yes?' I responded, turning round to the seated figure. Mrs Henderson looked me straight in the eye.

'I just wanted to say ...' She paused. I braced myself for the diatribe. It never came. 'I just wanted to say … thank you for today. We heard this week that my son, Ian, has AIDS. He got it from a contaminated blood transfusion for his haemophilia. We've been in tears all week. I didn't know whether I should come today. I felt dirty. The stigma of it ... all that stuff you read about God's punishment and the nasty things people say. It isn't Ian's fault, but it's just been terrible.'

Mrs Henderson stopped and looked up at me. She had tears in her eyes. 'How did you know?' she whispered. 'How did you know? It's as if what you shared today was just for me – and Ian too. Now I know that Ian can still belong here, and me too. But how did you know? How did you know?'

Mrs Henderson was now weeping openly. I sat beside her and put an arm round her shoulder. 'How did you know?' she sobbed. I didn't bother replying. There was nothing I could say. So I just cried along with Mrs Henderson. And I knew that a bad feeling and a bad day and a bad week had just got considerably better.[2]

Prayer

Today I pray for those afflicted with HIV and AIDS –
those who are living with a death sentence;
those who are living with the gift of life as best they can.
Bless those who are living and those who are dying,
and those who are struggling to make sense of dying
when there's still living to be done.

Today I pray for those who are seeking to alleviate the suffering
of people afflicted by HIV and AIDS –
those in the frontline of care;
those doing research.
Bless those who reach out in compassion
to offer hope where people have none,
to value life even when it is threatened by disease and death.

Today I pray for those who are involved in education
about HIV and AIDS –
for those who are at risk;
for those who are learning about tolerance.
Bless those who struggle with cultural norms,
who challenge fear, lifestyle and discrimination,
and all that would threaten fullness of life.

Today I pray for those who challenge the world's prejudices
against people with HIV and AIDS –
who, in whatever way, seek to create a more accepting humanity.
Bless those who wrestle with their own prejudices and judgements,
who, like me, have much to learn,
and much loving still to give to our common life.
Amen

Sources:

1. THE HOLY BIBLE, NEW INTERNATIONAL VERSION® NIV® Copyright © 1973, 1978, 1984 by International Bible Society® Used by permission. All rights reserved worldwide.

2. Adapted from 'How did you know?', from *Welcoming Each Wonder*, Tom Gordon, Wild Goose Publications, 2013

Coming in from the cold

Advent & Christmas resources for remembering the Bible with children and young people

Janet Lees

Introduction

The Remembered Bible method: beyond words

I've been using the remembered Bible method for over twenty years now. It all began after a period of study with Gerald West at the Institute for the Study of the Bible in Pietermaritzburg in 1994. Gerald's work is with texts: looking at interpretations that offer liberation to marginalised people. He calls this *'reading with'* others. But as a speech therapist I knew lots of people who would struggle to be 'reading with' so I began to work on oral interpretations that did not rely on reading a written text. This has become *'Remembering the Bible'* (or RB) – not rote learning but using remembered versions of the Bible narrative, which may be oral, visual or a combination, and developing interpretations through this approach that can be used by people of all ages and abilities. I've done two previous collections of this sort of thing, *Word of Mouth* and *Tell Me the Stories of Jesus* (Wild Goose Publications), which help to explain how to improvise or 'just go for it'.

Eight years ago I took this approach with me to Silcoates School when I became the Chaplain and introduced it to the children and young people with the aim that they might reclaim the Bible as their own book. Some of the results are shared in this material for Advent and Christmas. Much of it does not need to be used in a rigid and prescribed way. Try to get into the flow and see how it can release the remembered Bible in and with the people around you. Using RB is about merging ideas and hearing many voices.

Janet Lees

RESOURCES FOR ADVENT

Although Advent/Christmas is about the best-remembered season of all when it comes to 'Remembering the Bible', it can still be tricky. First of all, you need to decide what to do about Advent. In a school the term is likely to end before Christmas, which means Advent will be cut short if you stick to the traditional four weeks. You can accommodate this by merging weeks together to make maybe three weeks of Advent, or you can start a week earlier and have Advent 1 in the week before Advent Sunday, although this is also often national Anti-bullying Week.

If you go with three weeks of Advent, patriarchs, matriarchs and prophets can make Week 1, followed by John the Baptist for Week 2 and Mary for your final week.

Happy day

Advent God,
as we wait out these happy days
welcome us in from the draughty doorstep
of the tomb-lined garden
into the warmth of your company
to share the wine of your kin-dom.

Introductory words for Advent

Voice 1: Stories are told in many cultures.
In some a fire is kindled
and images are brought from dark corners
into the circle of warming flames.

(Advent candles are lit here, the number depending on the week or Sunday in Advent.)

Voice 2: In some a tree is planted
and people of all ages gather in its shade
to share the wisdom of youth and age.

(A cross is placed next to the candle/s.)

Voice 3: In some a book is opened
and words are collected together:
a source to feed many generations.

(An open Bible is placed alongside the candle/s and cross.)

Voice 1: O Fire-kindler

All voices: Ignite your truth in us.

Voice 2: O Tree-planter

All voices: Shade us with your love.

Voice 3: O Story-gatherer

All voices: Prompt us to act as one body.

Come to us in words and silence:
fill hearts and minds
with wonder and surprise
as we gather as your community.

Prayer for prophets in Advent

'Advent is about repentance. Why don't you tell them about that?'
– A boy, aged 13

About this time of year
prophets are appearing,
in the ups and downs of the market,
the talks about climate change, or the Euro,
the camps on pavements ...
In financial centres or shanty towns,
you may hear their voices
calling us back to God's standards,
the real 'gold standard',
reminding us to cherish the earth,

and think about our global responsibilities
and our real priorities.
Forgive us when, unmoved,
we fail to embrace the last-minute opportunities
that could transform us.
Help us to stay awake!
Forge us in the prophets' fire
that we can be remade as your people,
brighter and sharper than ever.

Advent people

The now common practice of remembering people by leaving flowers, and perhaps candles or soft toys, at the place of their unexpected death can surprise us. The experience of coming across such memorials, and also across social media sites remembering friends or relatives, is something children and young people have spoken to me about ...

Here we are, Advent people:
dead flowers on the pavement
the public mark of memories.

Here we are, Advent people:
pictures in my head
headlines ringing in my ears.

Here we are, Advent people:
waiting still
to be surprised by your coming
into this desperate world;
marvelling that this infant,
tiny, naked, vulnerable,
can be the means to make the world whole.

Advent prayer

On the pitch seagulls are waiting;
in the hedge small birds are waiting;
wait with us, Creator God.

In the lunch queue pupils are waiting;
in the car park parents are waiting;
wait with us, Jesus our friend.

In the library, knowledge is waiting;
in the classroom technology is waiting;
wait with us, Spirit of discovery.

And as we wait together,
may we not be limited to the passive waiting
of apathy and indifference,
but open us up to wait actively
with compassion and a thirst for justice
so that what we do as we wait today
may change tomorrow and give hope
to those for whom waiting seems hopeless.

John the Baptist in retirement

John the Baptist is an important figure to remember in Advent. As the forerunner of Jesus he introduces us to him and has an important ministry in his own right. I have some key props for remembering John the Baptist: a pot of honey – and a tin of fried grasshoppers. My mother won the tin of fried grasshoppers in a raffle when I was about 10 years old. I inherited it and have always used it for remembering John the Baptist (she didn't have a camel-hair coat so I couldn't inherit that).

Here's one of my sketches for adults about John the Baptist, who, as you will see in this version, didn't *get his head cut off, because he compromised in order to have a safer, more comfortable existence: something we can all relate to.*

When using this try to learn the words or retell it in your own way rather than just read it out.

The scene is the Nazarene Residential Home. Centre stage – and asleep on a chair with his TV supper (a jar of honey and a tin of fried grass-hoppers) on a tray in front of him – is the aged John the Baptist. He wakes up suddenly.

Oh, I must have dozed off. I keep doing that these days. I see you're still here. Me too. Oh look, the care worker has left me my usual supper – honey and locusts *(rubs his tummy)*. I must tell her sometime that it doesn't really agree with me these days. Repeats a bit, you know. I don't want to upset her though.

(He appears distracted.)

I see you're still here. Me too. I'm John. John the Baptist. Him they called 'the Baptiser'. Nice room, eh? Nice place. Not really what I expected in my old age. Well, I didn't really expect an old age, did you? I'd had a wild youth. All that desert survival stuff, insect-based diet, camel-hair garments *(scratches himself)*. I mean, I do understand that youth is like that. Just like today's young people – wild, eh? Think they're gonna change the world. Yeh – so did I.

(Nods off and then wakes up.)

You still here? Me too. I'm as surprised to find myself here as you are. But once Jesus came on the scene there were only two choices: early retirement or ... If I was going to keep my head things had to change. Challenging Roman soldiers was one thing but going head to head with Herod – that was just stupid. I had to back down, compromise.

(He seems to forget where he is.)

You still there? Me too. Still wondering 'What if?...' No, it's no good. This place is full of us: ex-Zealots, former Essenes and Nazarites, the odd ex-fish-erman or tax collector, former members of the People's Front for the Libera-tion of Judea. All the same: all wondering 'What if?...' I followed Jesus' career for a while. Tried to work out what he was up to. Even sent some of my fol-lowers after him to ask 'Are you the one, or should we expect another?' ...

(He dozes off again.)

About this time of year

By the time we get to weeks three or four of Advent we start to meet some angels.

Initially this prayer went with the construction of a huge angel figure made from a frame of chicken wire, papier mâché and cloth. Though not exactly the Angel of the North, *it was about 8 feet tall – so quite a sight – and welcomed people to our celebrations.*

If you are all out of chicken wire or the mess of papier mâché doesn't appeal to you, you could instead project photos of angels from art during the reading of this prayer, including the Angel of the North.

Unto us a birth is announced, new life is given, declaring change for individuals and communities; named Life-giver, Wonderful listener, Peacemaker; One of endless presence and hope-filled company ... (version of Isaiah 9:6–7)

About this time of year
there are angels visiting,
which is just as well
for those of us who
have slipped up or down.

They come with surprising news
in unlikely circumstances,
which is just as well
for those of us who
have to make difficult decisions.

They come with a message
of reassurance and hope,
which is just as well
for those of us who
are feeling hopeless or fearful.

You may be struggling
to believe in angels at all

but look closely at
the next message-bearer,
the next wound-healer,
the next hope-sharer
and you might find
your very own angel.

May God's love and peace
be a haven of security and hope
this Advent and Christmas.

Oral and written gospel: the Nativity

There is one important matter to consider when remembering the Christmas story, and that is the way in which it illustrates the relationship between the oral and written gospels.

Each of the four gospels begins with a different aspect of Nativity. Matthew and Luke have the birth narratives, Mark does not, beginning instead with John the Baptist and Jesus' rebirth at his baptism, and John has the cosmic Word of God.

The remembered Nativity, depicted in songs, plays and pictures, is usually a hybrid of Luke and Matthew with a few extras like innkeepers. There is nothing wrong with this. It is a legitimate expression of faith developed and retold by ordinary people. It is a form of the oral gospel and as such is quite a different genre to the written gospel, just as the mystery plays were a well-known genre in parts of Europe in the Middle Ages. Comparing the two may not be the most helpful thing but it can be a good idea to try to understand some of the important differences.

Because the written gospel is printed it has authority above that of the oral gospel. But in fact most scholars agree that the origins and veracity of the birth of Jesus recorded by Luke and Matthew are difficult to establish. Some scholars suggest there are aspects of eyewitness accounts, others think that they were all written with a political or theological purpose.

So, are the stories fiction? Again it is difficult to be definite about this as we do not know enough about the crucible of faith from which these narratives emerged. They clearly do have links to the body of Jewish scriptures and traditions. Whatever the truth behind the origins, they have remained central to a story two thousand years old. Like all old stories they change in the retelling. What is important is how they give life to people now.

The oral gospel has lasted for more than two thousand years, and has been developed and retold in myriad ways in different places and cultures. Sometimes the story emphasises the roles of the human characters, sometimes its animals are the focus. In this way the story is a kind of extended allegory and usually is used to affirm key Christian themes like welcome or support for the poor or God's total self-giving. All of these are important themes to reconsider at this time of year. It is my view that wherever the story is told, whether in songs, drama or pictures of whatever media, then it is told in memory of the One, and as such our human efforts to keep the oral gospel alive are to be commended.

Some examples of reworking the gospel at Christmas

About two thousand years later ... A decree went out that all the world should be taxed, which for some reason is never popular and was generally considered to be the fault of the bankers. This added to a mass movement of population that had been going on for some time, as poor people the world over tried to find some security and the squeezed middle tried to do the same (while the rich continued paying themselves huge bonuses). Somewhere amongst this mass of humanity, a small family of no account, a man and woman with an unplanned pregnancy, got inevitably caught up, and found themselves carried along in a desperate tide, to an insignificant city in an unremarkable country, there to depend on charity and handouts to survive the harshest conditions. It was as bad as this: the child of this homeless couple was born in a stable and laid in a manger. But should we have any sympathy for them, who were obvious Benefit cheats in the making and unwanted by anyone? Their only visitors were a bunch of tuneless carol singers, a group of out of work manual labourers and a small symposium of lost academics. 'A true story?' I hear you ask. I know only this: that it is as feasible today as it was two thousand years ago, and only faith, hope and love can make from this unlikely beginning a life-giving promise of peace on earth.

Or you could adapt something from today's news for your starting point, like this from December 2010:

> The great Christmas getaway was halted yesterday when Heathrow Airport, the UK's biggest, was closed due to adverse weather conditions. Hundreds of people had to spend the night in a cold Arrivals Hall and passengers complained of the lack of heating. A BAA spokesperson said that blankets and food had been handed out.
>
> There were also reports that a failed asylum seeker, known only as Mary, who was due to be deported from the UK yesterday with her fiancé, Joseph, gave birth in the left luggage area. The baby was placed in one of those metal trays you see going round and round on luggage carousels. The UK Border Agency refused to deny or confirm the claims that were reported by a startled collection of airport staff: cleaners, baggage-handlers and the like. When asked if the baby would be detained in the nearby Immigration Centre with his parents, a Government Minister said there would be a debate about children in detention in Parliament in the New Year.
>
> Three members of a UN delegation on their way to high-level talks and in transit through Heathrow tried to give the family some assistance. However, their gifts of gold, frankincense and myrrh were confiscated by security as being just the sort of thing that might be used to create a major security incident. They were told to go home by another route.
>
> Meanwhile, mobile phone footage, now circulating on YouTube, of Mary taken by other passengers is the only record we have of this event. She appears serene, and when asked said, 'I trust God.'

O come all ye faithful?: a sketch

Sometimes a sketch is just the thing. It needs to be fast and punchy and have some familiar aspects that folk can readily relate to. This one shows just how many traditional carols are linked to and influence our remembering of the Bible at Christmas. For it you will need three actors: Angel, Shepherd and Cow.

Shepherd and Angel enter, back to back, and bang into each other in the middle of the stage – they are surprised.

Angel: Watch out! Who are you and what are you doing?

Shepherd: *(use a local accent)* Oh by gum! I'm a shepherd of course and I'm watching my flock by night.

Angel: Well, you must be just the one I'm looking for.

Shepherd: Why? Who are you?

Angel: I'm the Angel of the Lord of course. Can't you tell?

Shepherd: No, how was I supposed to know?

Angel: Well – it's my glory shining all around.

Shepherd: *(scratches head)* If you say so *(sits down)*.

Angel: What are you doing now?

Shepherd: Like I said: watching my flock by night, all seated on the ground.

Angel: Well, shouldn't you be a bit more scared?

Shepherd: Scared – I'll have you know us shepherds are a brave and fearless lot.

Angel: What? Has not mighty dread seized your troubled mind?

Shepherd: I don't think so – weren't they a dodgy rock group that played here last year?

Angel: Well, do make an effort – I'm supposed to say 'Fear not!'

Shepherd: Well, go ahead – don't mind me.

Angel: *(a bit miffed)* Well, it don't really seem worth it now.

Shepherd: Oh, go on – I'm still listening.

Angel: Oh, all right. Glad tidings I bring of great joy.

Shepherd: That's nice. Who's getting that then?

Angel: You and all people.

Shepherd: Jolly good. What's it in aid of?

Angel: Unto you in David's town is born a Saviour.

Shepherd: Really, are you sure?

Angel: Yes, it's Christ the Lord.

Shepherd: How do you know?

Angel: *(getting cross)* Because *this* shall be a sign to you.

Shepherd: This?

Angel: Yes – you shall find the babe wrapped in swaddling clothes and lying in a manger.

At this point a cow enters behind them, backwards, and bangs into them.

Angel & shepherd: Watch out! What do you think you're doing?!

Cow: I'm an oxen standing by.

Angel: Standing by, standing by? What do you mean standing by *(smoothing down clothes)*?

Cow: I got this text. It says: 'Stand by, oxen.' It's from the Headmaster *(taps nose conspiratorially)*. So oxen standing by – that's me!

Shepherd: Where are you standing by?

Cow: In that lowly stable.

Shepherd: Which one?

Angel: That one with the baby away in the manger.

Shepherd: What's a baby doing away in a manger?

Cow: It's got no crib for a bed.

Shepherd: Poor thing, that can't be very comfortable. But you hanging about there, won't that wake the little baby up?

Cow: No, not this one: the cattle are lowing, the baby awakes, the little Lord Jesus no crying he makes.

Shepherd: That's amazing. How does it do that?

Angel: Little Jesus sweetly sleeps, sweetly sleeps, sleeps in comfort, slumbers deep.

Shepherd: Well, what are we going to do now?

Angel & cow: We will rock him rock him rock him.

Shepherd: We will what?

Angel & cow: We will rock him rock him rock him.

Shepherd: Has this turned into some sort of Bob Geldof Christmas single or something?

Cow: Why don't you come and look?

Angel: Yes, why don't you come and see the fur to keep him warm, snugly round his tiny form?

Shepherd: So when are we going then?

Angel: We'll go now.

Shepherd: Now, but it's come upon a midnight clear just now.

Angel: Yes, I know and can you hear those glorious songs of old?

Shepherd: I'm not sure – who is it anyway?

Angel: It's the other angels bending near to earth to touch their harps of gold.

Shepherd: I don't know, it all sounds bonkers to me. You couldn't make this stuff up, could you?

Cow: I do agree. I blame all those 19th-century carol writers myself.

Angel: Well, so do I really but it is a good story.

Shepherd: I agree – could we go somewhere warm and hear the rest?

Angel: Yes, that's a good idea. We'll try that stable over there.

Cow: What shall we say when we get to the door?

Shepherd: How about we want some figgy pudding?

All: And we won't go until we get some *(exit singing this)*.

Job appraisal: a sketch

Job appraisal is a common experience in many occupations – and certainly well known in staffrooms throughout the country! In this sketch Saint Peter is giving feedback to the Angel Gabriel … (This was written for Silcoates staff in December 2011.)

St Peter: Ah yes, I've got it here somewhere, sit down, sit down. Now then, we sent out questionnaires to everyone we could think of – members of the Church Triumphant and the Church Militant, even the Mormons, and to the Devil and the hoards of Hell. We even got a few responses from souls in Purgatory and one from Limbo – but we didn't count that.

Angel Gabriel: Why not?

St Peter: Theologians are currently debating whether or not Limbo really exists so it didn't seem fair to include that really. Anyway, as I was saying, we got all these back and I'm charged with giving you some feedback about this – after all, we all want to improve, don't we?

Angel Gabriel: Yes, of course, although this is the first appraisal I've had in over 2000 years.

St Peter: Exactly – well, things are going to change round here I can tell you. I mean, all that queuing at the Pearly Gates to get in before a bank holiday – that's got to stop – angels are going to have to be more flexible and work bank holidays from now on.

Angel Gabriel: They won't like it.

St Peter: Of course they won't but it's *your* job to communicate it to them.

Angel Gabriel: Thought it might be.

St Peter: Talking about communication, the survey suggests the need to improve yours. All this talking in old-fashioned language,

'Fear not' and stuff – people don't get it these days. What's wrong with 'Cool it'?

Angel Gabriel: I see, anything else?

St Peter: Yes, you need to be seen around more. I mean a couple of appearances in two thousand years. I mean you're not exactly working your socks off, are you?

Angel Gabriel: Well, there was that extra appearance in the trenches at Mons – don't forget that.

St Peter: I'm not really sure that a few shell-shocked Tommies and a deranged war poet can be considered reliable witnesses. Furthermore, your management of the Heavenly Host has been called into question.

Angel Gabriel: Has it? How do you mean?

St Peter: Well, all this 'Glory to God in the Highest' – it's not what people want these days. More 'Glory to God in the High Street' – can you manage that?

Angel Gabriel: I suppose so.

St Peter: And while you're at it, the gear and the name – all need updating – 'Angel Gabriel' is a bit last century. Couldn't we go for 'Gabe' and print it on a hoodie?

Angel Gabriel: A hoodie? Isn't that going a bit far?

St Peter: Ah, I see, I expected resistance, but not from you. Come now, we can outsource the angels you know. We've had several other bids – the England Rugby team – they don't seem to have much to do at the moment. Here's another from the *(local school)* Senior Management Team – yes, even them.

Angel Gabriel: OK, OK, I'll see what we can do. I'd better be heading back to Bethlehem now – got that annual gig in Shepherds' Fields tonight.

St Peter: Fine, fine – I seem to have a lot on my desk – sorry I can't join you – make it a good one.

(Angel Gabriel exits.)

Chocolate Advent challenge

Advent calendars of every theme possible – from superheroes to films to celebrity this and that – are available from about September onwards. Most have a chocolate connection. If you can keep your hands off the chocolate until December 1st, then here's a little challenge based around RB which can extend from the end of the autumn term up to Christmas Eve itself. Children can report back with their responses in the New Year when term begins again. The idea is to complete each sentence with a phrase of RB.

For this you will need: one fairtrade Advent Calendar, a pen or pencil, these pages.

For each day of Advent fill in the sentence with something you can remember about Jesus, for example:

Jesus who … spoke to fishermen.

Then reward yourself with a piece of chocolate from the Advent calendar.

1. Jesus who ………………………………………………………………

2. Jesus who ………………………………………………………………

3. Jesus who ………………………………………………………………

4. Jesus who ………………………………………………………………

5. Jesus who ………………………………………………………………

6. Jesus who ………………………………………………………………

7. Jesus who ………………………………………………………………

8. Jesus who ....

9. Jesus who ....

10. Jesus who ....

11. Jesus who ....

12. Jesus who ....

13. Jesus who ....

14. Jesus who ....

15. Jesus who ....

16. Jesus who ....

17. Jesus who ....

18. Jesus who ....

19. Jesus who ....

20. Jesus who ....

21. Jesus who ....

22. Jesus who ....

23. Jesus who ....

24. Jesus who ....

RESOURCES FOR CHRISTMAS

If you work in a school it's likely you will have started to celebrate Christmas before the end of Advent. If in a church or community project you may have more options (unless the situation is one where all the dates are already sewn up because 'we do it like this every year'). Try to break out of any ruts you might have got into with a bit of RB.

First and last Christmas

Remember that people's last Christmas may hold poignant memories, especially for those who have been bereaved.

On 12th December 2005, I went to Tavistock Square to stand by the spot where a Number 30 bus was blown apart by a bomb on 7th July that year. It was the first time I'd been to London since those events, which happened not far from where I used to work …

As I pass the spot
I see the flowers.
Dead now
they remind me of the
living
waiting
for the first Christmas,
remembering the last Christmas.

I recall the familiar stable scene:
halting shepherds;
voiceless angels;
the not-so-wise with their gifts.
That very first Christmas
in your imperfect world.

Christmas Christ,
we recall the events of the year,
knowing that only your vulnerable presence
can make the difference this first Christmas
to those bearing memories of the last Christmas.

Christmas every day

For this you need at least two voices. It's based on the pop song 'I wish it could be Christmas every day'. The person who reads that line needs to find a way of saying it with a slightly different emphasis each time.

I wish it could be Christmas every day.

Do you, do you really?

Yes, I wish it could be Christmas every day.

What, the whole lot?

Yes, I wish it could be Christmas every day.

Turkey and roast spuds and Christmas pud?

Yes, I wish it could be Christmas every day.

What, even sprouts?

Yes, I wish it could be Christmas every day.

The Queen's Speech?

Yes, I wish it could be Christmas every day.

Oh, I get it: it's the presents, isn't it?

Yes, I wish it could be Christmas every day.

Well, no one could afford that, could they?

Yes, I wish it could be Christmas every day.

You're bonkers you are – what, a present every day?

Yes, I wish it could be Christmas every day – think about it!

O Jesus,
let Christmas be every day.
Let it all happen as the angels said:
Glory to God in the highest and peace on earth.
Christ, what a Christmas that would be!

I have a message for you

When we first did this one at school, at the final assembly of the autumn term, everyone clapped. That raised the question: 'Should we be clapping a prayer?' Well, why not? Hands together and eyes closed is after all only one way to pray.

'I have a message for you,' said the angel.

It's not a film,
or a film of a book,
or a book, or a play,
but a message.

It's not satire or tragedy,
it's neither soap nor opera,
it's not a tweet or a text,
but a message.

It's not a snapchat,
or an instagram
or a YouTube clip,
but a message.

God has chosen you.
It's not a bit part
or a supporting role,
it's your whole life
that has attracted God's attention.
There are no lines to learn.
It's completely unscripted.
Just live your life
in tune with God's call
and in response to God's love
growing in you daily.

Listen, you can hear the message
echoing around the world:
'Glory to God in the highest:
peace on earth.'
Now you try.

Prayers for Nativity services

Dear Jesus,
when we think of your birthday
we get really excited.

Help us to enjoy Christmas
with our families and friends
and when we do to remember you
and others who, like you,
have nowhere to live this Christmas.
Help us to make a difference.

Dear Jesus,
with you to guide me
I'll give everything I can.
Help me to be willing and reliable –
even if some people are surprised!
May Christmas time be the biggest surprise ever
as we celebrate and remember your story
with those we love.

Don't be afraid (Luke 2:10)

'Don't be afraid' said the angel.

Don't cower in empty barns
or long-disused warehouses,
or inhabit pointless power towers
or palaces echoing with disappointment:
there's no need to be afraid.

Get out into the meadows of new growth,
the supermarkets of opportunity,
the gyms of health and well-being,
the factories of peace
and don't be afraid.

Stand on the corners of new meeting
or the platforms of new arrivals.
Cross the viaducts of new connections,
take the ferries of new horizons
but don't be afraid.

God moved into our street:
lives in our community,
goes to our school,
sits on the bus with us,
so don't be afraid.

Surprising

When the angels sang their song
announcing peace on earth,
it was surprising to the shepherds.
When the angel gave a message
to search out a baby in a manger,
it was surprising even to those familiar with farming.
This is a season of surprises.
May we who know the surprising story of angels and shepherds
be ready to learn from today's surprising news,
to look out for God's ways and Christ's presence,
in mangers or marginal places,
in stables or sheltered housing,
and be ready to join in the song of peace on earth.

Thinking of Christmas

When I'm lonely,
I think of Mary and Joseph,
who had nowhere to stay.

When I'm cold and tired,
I think of the shepherds,
out on the hills all night.

When I'm confused,
I think of the wise men,
not sure which way to go.

Wherever I am,
I try to think of Jesus,
born at Christmas,
because God loves you and me.

H is for homelessness

Homelessness is not just for Christmas but Christmas is an important time to think about it, and hopefully take some action by supporting a local project for homeless people.

Not enough

Depending on your ability, you could rap this one …

Not enough spaces, not enough places.
Not enough land, so we build on sand
and on floodplains.
Not enough profit, not enough gain.
So prices go up again and again.
Where are the rooms, the roofs, the walls,
the sound foundations and open doors?
Promises from this party or that:
too much stress, too little hope.
We are waiting, waiting, waiting.

(Repeat the first bit softly while the next part of the prayer is said.)

God of time and place,
this is our lament:
for those who need a new address.
Help us to address the issues so that
everyone has a warm welcome,
a roof over their heads
and the stability that comes with a proper home.

Living with us

The gospel storyteller recalls *'He came and lived with us and it was brilliant.'*

The word is out on the streets:
the word is that the door is open.
The word is being passed on:
the word is that all are welcome.
This word has been going around since the beginning,
but people can't quite seem to believe it.
The word is true: trust it.

Living Word, living with us,
may we be open to your grace and truth
and so doing open our hearts, our lives and our homes
to you and all who come in your name.
That would be really brilliant!

And lastly … looking forward

Of course not all of the stories are happy ones. Around this time there is also the Massacre of the Innocents to remember.

You'll need to insert the names of places where contemporary events reflect this story: there will be some – perhaps where families are fleeing persecution and misery in small boats by crossing difficult seas, or being herded across borders and kept in camps or being trafficked by people-smugglers. Whatever it is, remember it – ask the young people to make suggestions.

I'm not looking forward to the Massacre of the Innocents.
I don't want to hear Rachel weep again,
to see the mothers cradling their dead children,
their faces torn apart by tragedy and grief.

I'm not a media mogul getting rich on world exclusives,
or a weary newsreader on a 24-hour shift to spread the word,
but I have seen their scenes before:
in Aleppo, Darfur, Kashmir, Tavistock Square *(insert examples …)*
and I need to know they are remembered
by God and humanity
bridging the worlds of loss and centuries of devastation,
making it possible that 'they all shall be one'.

Coming in from the cold

As we wrap up warm
and listen again to the Christmas story,
may the baby in the manger
remind us that even the smallest have a place,
even the most vulnerable are valuable,
and that God can surprise us any day.
May children and young people
be the heralds of good news for us this season,
as, coming in from the cold margins of our world,
we worship together, singing Glory to God and peace on earth.

About the authors

Sarah Agnew is a storyteller, poet and minister in the Uniting Church in Australia, who leads worship, workshops and retreats with people in many places.

Nancy Cocks is a former Deputy Warden of Iona Abbey, after which she took up the post of professor at Atlantic School of Theology in Halifax, Nova Scotia and then served as minister of St John's Presbyterian Church in Medicine Hat, Alberta before retirement. Nancy is the author of several books, including *Invisible We See You* and *Growing Up With God* (Wild Goose).

Tom Gordon is a former hospice chaplain, a storyteller, a member of the Iona Community and the author of several books, including *The Very Life of Life* (Wild Goose, 2018).

Kes Grant is an unorthodox Church of England priest. She has been a hospital chaplain and a school chaplain.

Janet Lees is a URC minister and a speech therapist, and has been Chaplain at Silcoates School in Wakefield since 2010. She is the author of *Word of Mouth: Using the Remembered Bible for Building Community*, and *Tell Me the Stories of Jesus: A Companion to the Remembered Bible* (Wild Goose).

Rebeka Maples is Director of Spiritual Formation for local pastors in Course of Study at the Methodist Theological School in Ohio. She retired from parish ministry after serving Methodist churches in England and the U.S., but continues working with clergy and spiritual directors in various ecumenical contexts. Her inspiration comes from nature and the arts, with an eye for the holy wherever it may appear. She is a member of Spiritual Directors International and an associate member of the Iona Community.

Stephen J Maunder is a Methodist presbyter who is in ministry in Oxford.

Joy Mead is a member of the Iona Community and the author of *The One Loaf, A Telling Place, Making Peace in Practice and Poetry, Where Are the Altars?, A Way of Knowing, Walking Our Story, Glimpsed in Passing* and *Words and Wonderings*. She leads creative writing groups, and has been involved in development education and justice and peace work.

Thom M Shuman serves as a semi-retired pastor. Committed to non-violence, he supports justice for immigrants, refugees, and people with mental illness. He is an associate of the Iona Community, and the author of several books and downloads, including *The Soft Petals of Grace* (Wild Goose).

Jan Sutch Pickard is a former Warden of Iona Abbey, a storyteller, liturgist and Methodist lay preacher. She has twice served as a peace monitor with the Ecumenical Accompaniment Programme in Palestine and Israel. She is the author of several books, including *A Pocket Full of Crumbs* (Wild Goose).

Wild Goose Publications is part of the Iona Community

- An ecumenical movement of men and women from different walks of life and different traditions in the Christian church
- Committed to the gospel of Jesus Christ, and to following where that leads, even into the unknown
- Engaged together, and with people of goodwill across the world, in acting, reflecting and praying for justice, peace and the integrity of creation
- Convinced that the inclusive community we seek must be embodied in the community we practise

Together with our staff, we are responsible for:

- Our islands residential centres of Iona Abbey, the MacLeod Centre on Iona, and Camas Adventure Centre on the Ross of Mull

and in Glasgow:

- The administration of the Community
- Our work with young people
- Our publishing house, Wild Goose Publications
- Our association in the revitalising of worship with the Wild Goose Resource Group

The Iona Community was founded in Glasgow in 1938 by George MacLeod, minister, visionary and prophetic witness for peace, in the context of the poverty and despair of the Depression. Its original task of rebuilding the monastic ruins of Iona Abbey became a sign of hopeful rebuilding of community in Scotland and beyond. Today, we are about 280 Members, mostly in Britain, and 1500 Associate Members, with 1400 Friends worldwide. Together and apart, 'we follow the light we have, and pray for more light'.

For information on the Iona Community contact:
The Iona Community, 21 Carlton Court,
Glasgow G5 9JP, UK. Phone: 0141 429 7281
e-mail: admin@iona.org.uk; web: www.iona.org.uk

For enquiries about visiting Iona, please contact:
Iona Abbey, Isle of Iona, Argyll PA76 6SN, UK. Phone: 01681 700404
e-mail: ionacomm@iona.org.uk

Wild Goose Publications, the publishing house of the Iona Community established in the Celtic Christian tradition of Saint Columba, produces books, e-books, CDs and digital downloads on:

- holistic spirituality
- social justice
- political and peace issues
- healing
- innovative approaches to worship
- song in worship, including the work of the Wild Goose Resource Group
- material for meditation and reflection

For more information:

Wild Goose Publications
The Iona Community
21 Carlton Court, Glasgow, G5 9JP, UK

Tel. +44 (0)141 429 7281
e-mail: admin@ionabooks.com

or visit our website at
www.ionabooks.com
for details of all our products and online sales